GRADE

8

W9-BEV-030

ISBN-13: 978-1-4190-9901-4
ISBN-10: 1-4190-9901-9

©2008 Harcourt Achieve Inc.
All rights reserved. This book is intended for classroom use and is not for resale or distribution. Each blackline master in this book may be reproduced, with the copyright notice, without permission from the Publisher. Reproduction for an entire school or district is prohibited. No other part of this publication may be reproduced or transmitted in any form or by any means, electronic or mechanical, including photocopying, recording, taping, or any information storage and retrieval system, without permission in writing from the Publisher. Contact: Paralegal Department, 6277 Sea Harbor Drive, Orlando, FL 32887.

Steck-Vaughn is a trademark of Harcourt Achieve Inc.

The paper used in this book comes from sustainable resources.

Steck Vaughn™
A Harcourt Achieve Imprint

Printed in the United States of America.
1 2 3 4 5 6 7 8   862   14 13 12 11 10 09 08 07

www.HarcourtSchoolSupply.com

Core Skills Writing
Grade 8

Unit 1: Laying the Foundation

Unit 2: Building Sentences

© Harcourt Achieve Inc. All rights reserved.

Unit 3: Building Paragraphs

Unit 4: Writing Forms

Blackline Masters

Introduction

Writing is one of the core skills necessary for success in school and in life. The better writer a person is, the better that person can communicate with others. Good writing is a skill acquired through guidance, practice, and self-evaluation. This book provides guidance for success in different writing formats. This book also provides many opportunities for writing practice. Finally, this book encourages writers to examine their own work and judge its qualities and flaws.

Clear writing and clear speaking are products of clear thinking. Clear thinking is a product of good organization of ideas. Good organization is a product of careful planning. One good way to plan is through graphic organizers.

- In this book, different kinds of graphic organizers are provided for students to plan their writing.
- One kind of graphic organizer, emphasized in Unit 2, allows writers to "see" their writing clearly.
- By "seeing" their writing, students can more easily determine how the different parts of a sentence work together to produce a clear expression of their main idea.
- This kind of graphic organizer allows students a more visual and tactile appreciation of their writing. It also appeals to multiple intelligences.

Language Arts Standards

The National Council of Teachers of English (NCTE) believes that "all students must have the opportunities and resources to develop the language skills they need to pursue life's goals and to participate fully as informed, productive members of society." The NCTE also feels that students must "apply a wide range of strategies as they write and use different writing process elements appropriately to communicate with different audiences for a variety of purposes."

The Skills Correlation Chart on page 7 allows easy location of these skills and strategies in the book.

Organization

This book is divided into four units. Each unit builds upon earlier units. Using this scaffolded approach, writing becomes like construction. This book can help to build better writers.

- **Unit 1: Laying the Foundation** addresses basic concepts of writing, such as good writing traits and the process of writing.
- **Unit 2: Building Sentences** emphasizes the act of writing. Writers first deal with the main idea of a sentence and then expand sentences by adding other parts of speech. By using graphic organizers, writers can visualize their sentences clearly.
- **Unit 3: Building Paragraphs** focuses on the structure and content of a well-written paragraph. Writers also learn about revising, proofreading, and self-evaluation in this unit.
- **Unit 4: Writing Forms** provides guidance and practice writing in different formats such as narration, description, persuasion, and informative reports.

Write Away

For too many students, writing is a struggle or a pain. They may not realize the benefits of being a good writer, or they may not care. This book tries to reach out to all writers with a light tone and an approach that allows students to "see" their writing in a new light. Writing does not have to be a chore. It can be fun. Students just have to be reminded that good writing can be their golden ticket to success in school and life.

www.harcourtschoolsupply.com
© Harcourt Achieve Inc. All rights reserved.

Core Skills Writing 8, SV 9781419099014

Features

The title clearly identifies the skill.

Bullets highlight important points of the skill.

Examples model the skill.

Students creatively apply the skill in **Write Away.**

The information box at the top of each page explains the skill in an interesting and lively way. Informal language encourages active participation.

A writing activity checks students' understanding.

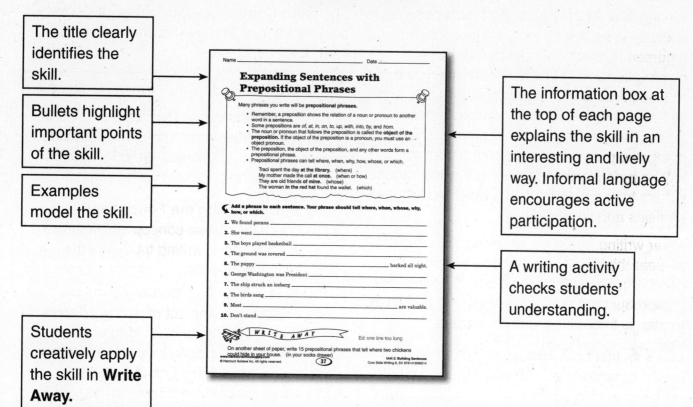

Checklists guide students through the writing process.

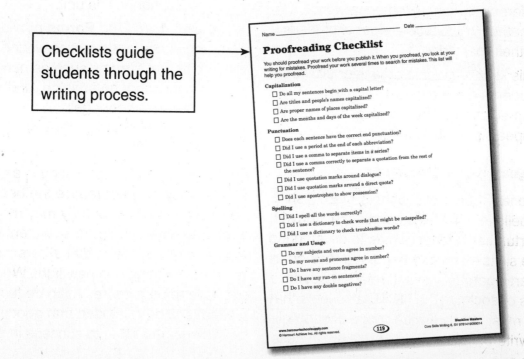

Features

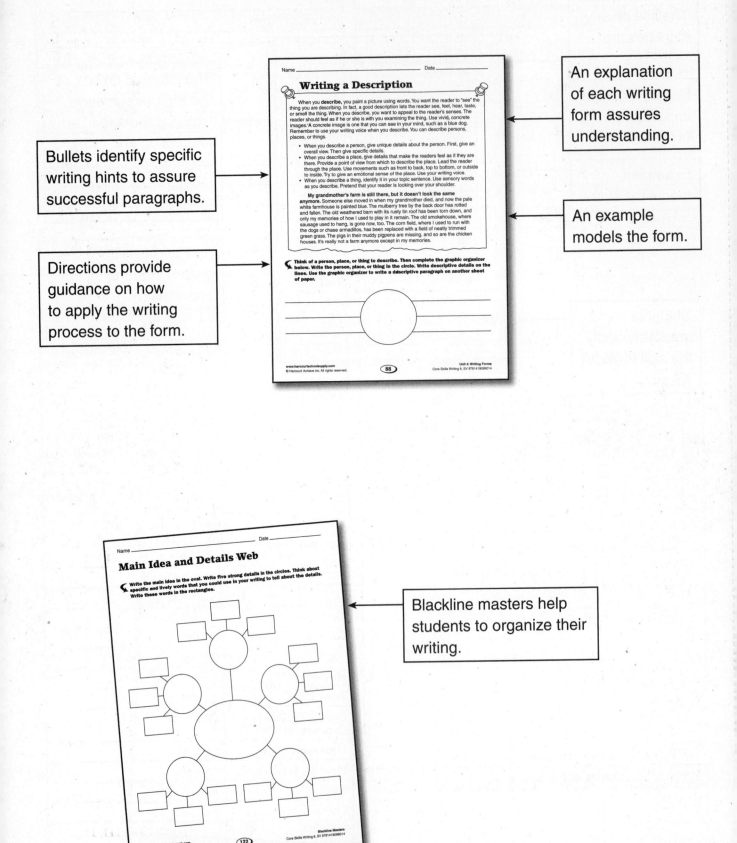

An explanation of each writing form assures understanding.

Bullets identify specific writing hints to assure successful paragraphs.

An example models the form.

Directions provide guidance on how to apply the writing process to the form.

Blackline masters help students to organize their writing.

www.harcourtschoolsupply.com
© Harcourt Achieve Inc. All rights reserved.

Features
Core Skills Writing 8, SV 9781419099014

Skills Correlation

Skill	Page
Vocabulary	
Word Choice	20, 31, 32, 33, 54, 57, 58, 59
Figurative Language	60, 91, 92
Sentences	
Word Order in Sentences	61
Recognizing Sentences and Sentence Types	50, 51, 52, 54
Main Idea of Sentence	24, 30
Subjects and Predicates	24, 25, 26, 27, 28, 29, 30, 44, 45, 49
Compound/Complex Sentences	52
Sentence Combining	61, 62, 64
Sentence Fragments	64
Run-on Sentences	65, 66
Clauses and Phrases	36, 37, 38, 39, 40, 41, 46, 47, 48, 49
Independent and Dependent Clauses	36, 45, 46, 47, 48
Compound Subjects and Predicates	44, 45
Objects	26, 30, 42
Predicate Nominatives and Predicate Adjectives	28, 29, 30
Sentence Variety	57, 58, 59, 61, 62, 63
Grammar and Usage	
Common and Proper Nouns	13
Singular and Plural Nouns	13
Possessive Nouns	13
Verbs and Verb Tense	14, 56
Subject-Verb Agreement	25, 45
Verb Phrases	27, 30
Active and Passive Voice Verbs	14, 55
Pronouns	13
Adjectives	15, 29, 31, 32, 33, 35, 38, 48, 57, 58, 59
Adverbs	15, 34, 38, 48
Prepositions	16, 36, 37, 38, 49
Prepositional Phrases	36, 37, 38, 49
Conjunctions	16, 36, 43, 46, 47, 48, 49, 53, 54
Verbals: Gerunds, Infinitives, Participles	39, 40, 41
Capitalization and Punctuation	
Capitalization: First Word in Sentence	23
Capitalization: Proper Nouns	13
End Punctuation	50, 51
Commas	53, 54, 66
Quotation Marks	90, 109

Skill	Page
Composition	
Expanding Sentences	31, 32, 33, 34, 35, 36, 37, 38, 39, 40, 42, 43, 44, 45, 46, 47, 48, 49
Paragraphs; Topic Sentence (main idea)	70, 71, 72, 75, 77, 122
Paragraphs: Supporting Details	70, 71, 73, 77, 122
Paragraph: Concluding Sentence	70, 71, 74
Order in Paragraphs	70, 79
Writing Process:	
Audience	10, 11, 17, 20, 75, 76, 100, 115, 116
Purpose	11, 17, 19, 33, 89, 93, 95, 101, 104, 106, 114, 115, 116
Voice	20, 33, 75, 87, 88, 89, 100, 108, 117
Prewriting and Brainstorming	17, 73, 75, 77, 98, 104, 115, 116
Topic	17, 19, 22, 70, 71, 72, 73, 75, 76, 77, 78, 83, 93, 94, 96, 104, 105, 107, 108, 112, 113, 114
Organization and Form	11, 19, 77, 78, 79, 80, 81, 82, 88, 89, 90, 91, 92, 93, 94, 95, 96, 97, 98, 99, 100, 101, 102, 103, 104, 105, 106, 107, 108, 109, 110, 111, 112, 113, 114, 121, 122, 123, 124
Outlining	112
Note Taking	108, 109
Drafting	17, 18, 22, 68, 86, 105, 114
Revising and Proofreading	18, 21, 22, 64, 65, 66, 69, 84, 85, 87, 114, 119, 120, 121
Publishing	18, 21, 86, 118
Types of Writing:	
Description	57, 58, 59, 88
Narration	89, 90
Poetry	91, 92
How-to	79
Persuasion	99, 100, 101
Comparing and Contrasting	80, 97, 98
Cause and Effect	81, 124
Problem and Solution	82, 124
Summary	78, 108, 123
Literary Response	102, 103
Informative Report	107, 108, 109, 110, 111, 112, 113, 114
Writing for Tests	104, 105, 106
Five-Paragraph Essay	93, 94, 95, 96

© Harcourt Achieve Inc. All rights reserved.

Writing Rubric

Score of 4
The student:

- clearly and completely addresses the writing task,
- demonstrates an understanding of the purpose for writing,
- maintains a single focus,
- presents a main idea supported by relevant details,
- uses paragraphs to organize main ideas and supporting ideas under the umbrella of a thesis statement,
- presents content in a logical order and sequence,
- uses variety in sentence types, beginnings, and lengths,
- chooses the correct writing pattern and form to communicate ideas clearly,
- clearly portrays feelings through voice and word choice,
- uses language appropriate to the writing task, such as language rich in sensory details in a descriptive passage,
- uses vocabulary to suit purpose and audience,
- summarizes main ideas in a concluding paragraph when appropriate,
- establishes and defends a position in a persuasive paragraph, and
- has few or no errors in the standard rules of English grammar, punctuation, capitalization, and spelling.

Score of 3
The student:

- generally follows the criteria described above, and
- has some errors in the standard rules of English grammar, punctuation, capitalization, and spelling, but not enough to impair the reader's comprehension.

Score of 2
The student:

- marginally follows the criteria described above, and
- has several errors in the standard rules of English grammar, punctuation, capitalization, and spelling that may impair a reader's comprehension.

Score of 1
The student:

- fails to follow the criteria described above, and
- has many errors in the standard rules of English grammar, punctuation, capitalization, and spelling that impair a reader's comprehension.

Why Write?

Are you a writer? Do you like to write? Many people say they don't like to write. They think they can speak everything they need to communicate. With all the cell phones in use now, maybe they are right. But sometimes writing is better than talking. Even e-mail and instant messaging require some sort of writing. Why is writing better than talking?

- When you write, you have more time to think about your ideas.
- You can organize your ideas better when you write them down.
- You can make your ideas more permanent by writing them on paper or storing them in a computer.
- Writing takes your place when you are not there to talk.

In fact, writing is really much like talking. When you write or talk, you use ideas. You use the different parts of speech. You often use complete sentences. And your goal is the same for both methods—to communicate with others. Writing can be fun, too. Just think, in twenty or thirty years, a phone conversation will be long gone, but you can read something you wrote in the eighth grade. What do you think you will be like in twenty or thirty years? Why not write it down?

Darken the circle by the answer that best completes each sentence.

1. You can take time to _____ before you write your ideas on paper.

   (A) send an e-mail   (B) find your pen

   (C) think more   (D) play a CD

2. When you write, you can take time to _____ your ideas better.

   (A) forget   (B) change

   (C) organize   (D) erase

3. Your ideas are _____ if you write them on paper.

   (A) dumber   (B) more permanent

   (C) funnier   (D) more intelligent

4. Writing can take your _____ when you aren't available to speak.

   (A) place   (B) lunch

   (C) money   (D) time

W R I T E   A W A Y

Do you like talking or writing better? Think about the question for a while. Discuss your ideas with a friend or family member. Then, write a few sentences to tell which you like better and why.

_____

_____

_____

_____

_____

_____

What to Write

Have you ever sat and watched letters coming out of the end of your pen or pencil? Try it. They appear almost magically on the paper, and soon you've written something. But what you've written may not make any sense. To be a good writer, you have to think about what you write. Sometimes you have a report to write. Sometimes you must give someone directions. Sometimes you want to jot down a list or compose a song or rap. There are lots of things you can write. Before you do, though, you should make three decisions.

1. **Who is your audience?** Your audience is your reader. But who will your audience be? Are you writing for yourself? Your friends or family? A teacher? The community? Before you write, ask yourself questions to target your audience.

   - Who will read what I write?
   - What do I know about these people?
   - Why do I want these people to care about my writing?
   - What do I have to say to these people?
   - Am I writing opinions or facts?
   - Will my writing be funny or serious, happy or sad?

   The more you know about your audience, the better you can target your readers.

Name a possible audience for each piece of writing.

1. your opinions about a new movie

   _____

2. a report about traffic problems

   Town hall

3. an invitation to a dance

   _____

4. a report about volcanoes

   classmates

5. a humorous story about a family member

   family

6. an election speech

   people 18 and up

W R I T E   A W A Y

Would a letter you write to your representative in Congress be different from a letter you write to a relative? How would the letters be different? Write a few sentences about your ideas.

When writing to a member of congres you would write in a formal manner. If writing to a relative you would write in a regular or semi-formal way.

What to Write, page 2

2. **Why are you writing?** Before you write, you must choose a **purpose,** or goal, for your writing. If you don't, you won't really know why you're writing, and neither will your readers. Writers have four main purposes:

   - to **express** personal feelings, ideas, or experiences (diary, journal, opinions)
   - to **inform** (facts, statistics, report, research paper)
   - to **entertain** others (story, poem, song, joke)
   - to **persuade** others (speech, argument, book review)

3. **How will you organize your writing?** Your audience and your purpose determine your organization. To be an effective writer, you must choose the correct form to achieve your purpose. This book presents many forms you can use to write.

What purpose would you use to write each of the following? Darken the circle by your choice.

1. a funny story about a singing dog

   (A) express   (B) entertain

   (C) persuade   (D) inform

2. a report about World War II

   (A) express   (B) entertain

   (C) persuade   (D) inform

3. your feelings about someone who has died

   (A) express   (B) entertain

   (C) persuade   (D) inform

4. a TV commercial for a new product

   (A) express   (B) entertain

   (C) persuade   (D) inform

WRITE AWAY

You want to use your savings to buy an MP3 player. How can you get your wish? Write a few sentences to persuade your parents or guardians.

What purpose would you use? _persuade_

Who would your audience be? _parents_

_____

_____

_____

_____

_____

_____

_____

Keeping a Journal

Jour is a French word that means "day." A **journal** is a record of daily events. In a journal, you can write about your experiences, ideas, thoughts, and feelings. You can write stories or poems in your journal. You can draw pictures. You can do anything you want in your journal because it's your special place. And journals can be fun to read when you get older. You can make your journal better by doing these things.

- Write the date.
- Write about important events that happened today.
- Tell why the events are important to you.
- Write poems, songs, or stories about the events and illustrate them.

Here's a sample:

October 26, 2007 Today a friend told me that a girl I knew in elementary school is in the hospital. She was in a bicycle accident and was not wearing a helmet. The doctor says she's going to be OK, but it is very scary. I ride my bike all the time, and I need to remember to wear my helmet.

Of all the things that happened to you today, which one will likely be the most memorable? Write about it in a short journal entry. Use another sheet of paper if necessary.

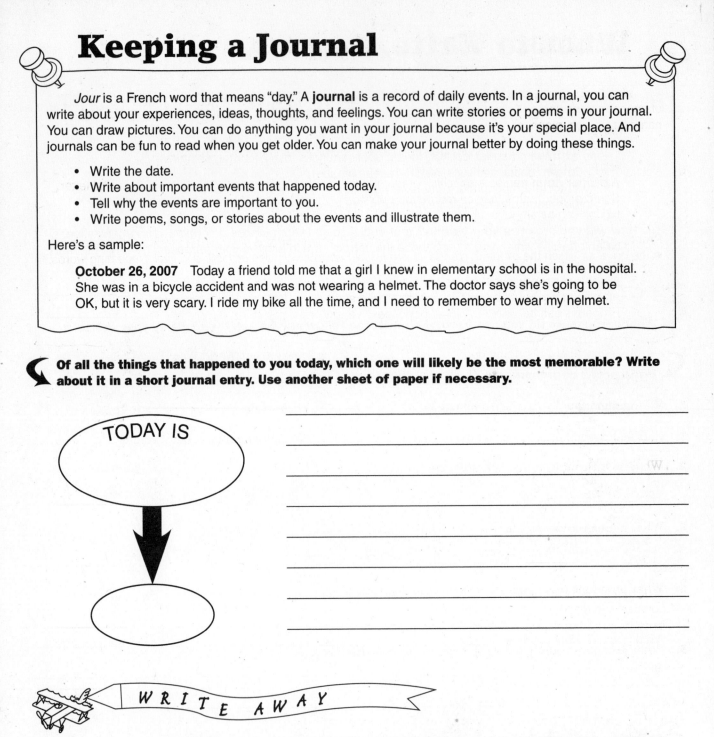

TODAY IS

WRITE AWAY

Do you keep a journal? If not, why not start one? You can use notebook paper or a notebook. Write the date. Write your feelings and ideas. Write poems and stories about your daily life. Writing your personal feelings can help you understand them better.

© Harcourt Achieve Inc. All rights reserved.
Core Skills Writing 8, SV 9781419099014

Primary Parts of Speech

When you write, you use the parts of speech to build your sentences. Two of the most important parts of speech are **nouns** and **pronouns.** Nouns and pronouns are used for naming. A noun is a word that names a person, place, or thing.

- A **common noun** names any person, place, or thing. A common noun begins with a small letter.   (dog, state, park)
- A **proper noun** names a specific person, place, or thing. A proper noun begins with a capital letter. Some proper nouns may be more than one word.   (Lassie, Nevada, Yosemite National Park)
- Nouns can be singular, plural, or possessive.   (cat, cats, cat's)

Pronouns take the place of nouns. Be sure the pronoun's **antecedent** is clear to the reader. The antecedent is the noun for which the pronoun stands. (**Angela** sold **her** stereo.) Use pronouns to avoid repeating words.

- A **subject pronoun** is used as the subject of a sentence.   (I, we, they, he, she, who)
- An **object pronoun** is used as the object of a sentence.   (me, us, them, him, her, whom)
- Pronouns can be singular, plural, or possessive.   (it, they, my)

Write nouns or pronouns to fit each writing need.

1. What nouns could you use to write about a mall?

_____

2. What nouns could you use to write about a truck?

_____

3. What nouns could you use to write about a book?

_____

4. What pronouns could you use to write about yourself?

_____

5. What pronouns could you use to write about your friends or family?

_____

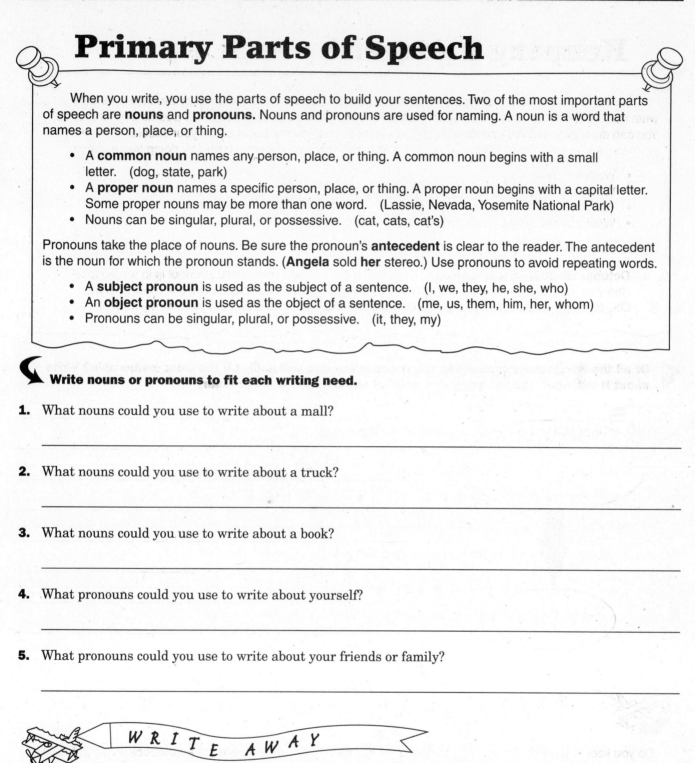

W R I T E   A W A Y

On another sheet of paper, write a list of twenty nouns. Beside each noun, write a pronoun that could be used to describe it. The noun would be used as the antecedent for the pronoun.

© Harcourt Achieve Inc. All rights reserved.
13

Primary Parts of Speech, page 2

A **verb** is another important part of speech. A verb shows action or connects the subject to another word in a sentence. Verbs can be **action verbs, linking verbs,** or **helping verbs.** Verbs can be singular or plural. They can be active or passive.

Verbs are also used to tell the time something is happening. The time a verb shows is called **verb tense.**

- A present tense verb tells what is happening now.   (help)
- A past tense verb tells what happened in the past.   (helped)
- A future tense verb tells what will happen in the future.   (will help)

Write verbs to fit each writing need.

1. What verbs could you use to write about cleaning the house?

_____

2. What verbs could you use to write about what you do on weekends?

_____

3. What verbs could you use to write about playing a sport?

_____

4. What verbs could you use to write about making music?

_____

5. What verbs could you use to write about a trip last year?

_____

6. What verbs could you use to write about a new CD that will be released next week?

_____

WRITE AWAY

Often, many verbs refer to a single action. What are some verbs that refer to moving using your feet? (jog) On another sheet of paper, write a list of all the verbs you can think of. Refer to this list as you write.

Modifiers

Adjectives and **adverbs** are two more parts of speech. Adjectives and adverbs are **modifiers**. A modifier is a word or group of words that modifies, or changes, the meaning of another word.

mule   ➡️   **singing** mule

- An adjective modifies a noun or pronoun.

  green grass   **silly** song   **lucky** him

- An adverb modifies a verb, an adjective, or another adverb.

  sat **quietly**   **very** tall   **quite** bravely

Write adjectives or adverbs to fit each writing need.

1. What adjectives could you use to write about the ocean?

_____

2. What adjectives could you use to write about your neighborhood?

_____

3. What adjectives could you use to write about the sky?

_____

4. What adverbs could you use to write about the way you sing?

_____

5. What adverbs could you use to write about the way old people move?

_____

6. What adverbs could you use to write about the way cats behave?

_____

WRITE AWAY

On another sheet of paper, draw a picture. Then write at least six sentences that describe your picture. Underline the adjectives and circle the adverbs in your sentences.

Connectives

Conjunctions and prepositions are two more parts of speech. Conjunctions and prepositions are **connectives.** Connectives join parts of a sentence.

- A conjunction connects words or groups of words.
- A **coordinate conjunction** joins words of equal rank. Some coordinate conjunctions are *and, or, but,* and *yet.*
- A **subordinate conjunction** joins groups of words of unequal rank. Some subordinate conjunctions are *because, since, though, before, that,* and *which.*

> here **and** there   true **or** false
> I returned the book **after** the library closed.

- A preposition shows the relation of a noun or pronoun to another word in a sentence. Some common prepositions are *of, at, in, on, to, up, near, from, by,* and *into.*

> Lava flowed **down** the side **of** the volcano.

Write a coordinate or subordinate conjunction to complete each sentence.

1. The wind off the ocean was cold, _____ Emily did not want to go in yet.

2. _____ the moon came up, the wind died down a bit.

3. The moonlight glinted on the waves, _____ Emily took in the beauty of the scene.

4. She did not want to go home _____ the beach vacation was over.

5. She thought she might become a beach bum, _____ she might become a famous surfer.

6. _____ it started to rain, Emily went into the beach house.

Write two prepositions that have a meaning similar to the given word.

7. by _____

8. below _____

WRITE AWAY

Think of prepositions that tell a location, such as *near* or *above.* Write as many prepositions as you can on another sheet of paper. Include each preposition in a phrase, such as **near** *the cave* and **above** *the bookshelf.*

The Writing Process

Have you ever started to write, and then just sat there and stared at a blank sheet of paper? Maybe you thought that words would hop onto the page from your pen, run around for a bit, and settle into place. Let's face it—sometimes you just can't think of anything to write. Don't despair. Many people have the same problem. Luckily, these steps can help you fill that blank paper with wonderful words.

1. Prewriting

Prewriting is sometimes called **brainstorming.** In this step you think about what and why you are writing. You choose a purpose and an audience. You choose a **topic** and make a list of your ideas. Then you organize your ideas so they make sense. Many writers use outlines or graphic organizers. The Prewriting Survey on pages 115 and 116 can help you plan your writing.

Pretend you ate a bag of chocolate-covered ants. You decide to write about it in your journal. Use the organizer to help you prewrite.

Nouns I might use: _____

Verbs I might use: _____

Adjectives I might use: _____

Adverbs I might use: _____

2. Drafting

In the drafting step, you get your ideas on paper. You can write words, ideas, or sentences. Some parts of the draft may have too little information. Other parts may have too much. You'll usually have grammar errors in this step of the writing process. But that's OK! A draft isn't supposed to be perfect. You just want to get your ideas on paper. You concentrate on what you want to say. You can fix your mistakes later.

Write a sentence you might include in your journal about eating chocolate-covered ants. Use some of the words you wrote above.

_____

_____

_____

_____

_____

_____

_____

_____

_____

The Writing Process, page 2

3. Revising

Revising means "seeing again." In the revising step, you "see" your draft again. If you have time, go away from the writing for a day or two. When you come back to it, read your work carefully to be sure it makes sense. You may find new ways to arrange your ideas. You can add or remove details to make the writing clearer. Try reading your writing aloud. Then you can often <u>hear</u> problems. Ask someone else to read your work and give you suggestions for improvement.

➤ **Use your sentence from page 17. Think about your sentence for a while. Then write the sentence again using different words or a different order.**

_____

_____

4. Proofreading

When you proofread, you read your writing carefully to find mistakes. You should read your work several times. Remember, you are looking for mistakes. Again, try reading it aloud. Use the Proofreading Checklist on page 119 as a guide. A list of Proofreading Marks can be found on page 120.

➤ **Proofread the following sentence. Make corrections. Then write the corrected sentence on the line.**

My families vacashun to the Painted Dessert endid in disastor.

_____

5. Publishing

Publishing your writing is fun. Publishing means "to make public." You can present your writing to your teacher, to your friends, to your family, or to the community. You can read it orally, post it on a Web site, or make it into a book. First, make a clean copy of your writing. You can hand write it or type it on the computer. Then, add pictures, a cover, and a title page if you like. Now the writing is ready to share!

➤ **Suppose you decide to write a book about chocolate-covered ants. Think of a title, and then design a title page for your book. Use another sheet of paper.**

WRITE AWAY

Think of different ways you can publish your writing. Write a list of your ideas below. Which way is most appealing to you? Why?

_____   _____

_____   _____

_____   _____

_____   _____

© Harcourt Achieve Inc. All rights reserved.
18

The Seven Traits of Good Writing

When you write, you have a **purpose,** or reason, for writing.

- You might want to express your feelings or opinions.
- You might want to inform or entertain your reader.
- You might try to convince your reader to do something or think a certain way.

There are seven **writing traits,** or skills, that can help you achieve your purpose. These writing traits can help you become a better writer.

1. **Ideas**
   You write about your **ideas,** or thoughts, on a topic. When you write, be sure that the readers understand your message. You want them to be interested in your message, too. So be sure your ideas make sense. Include enough details to make your ideas clear to the reader. Good ideas show good thinking.

2. **Organization**
   The **organization** of your writing is the way you group your ideas and details.

   - First, choose the correct form of writing for your purpose. E-mail messages, letters, essays, stories, reports, and journals are some writing forms.
   - Next, your writing needs good structure. Write your ideas in a logical order. Do you have a beginning, a middle, and an end? Do your paragraphs have strong topic sentences?
   - Finally, check your very first sentence. Is it boring, or does it grab the reader's attention? If it's interesting, the reader will keep reading. You've hooked the reader. That's important! Where would a writer be without a reader?

Answer each question.

1. You want to write about what life will be like fifty years from now. What are some ideas you could include?

   _____

   _____

2. What form of organization would you choose to tell about life in the future? Would you write a report? A story? A letter? Identify the form you would use.

   _____

   _____

WRITE AWAY

How is a letter like an e-mail message? How are they different? Brainstorm your ideas with a friend or family member. Then write two or three sentences about your ideas.

_____

_____

_____

The Seven Traits of Good Writing, page 2

3. Voice

When you talk, people can usually tell by your voice how you feel. They know if you are happy, sad, or angry. As a writer, you may want to let your reader know what you are feeling, too. You can show these feelings through the words you choose and the sentences you write. You use a writing **voice**. To share a happy feeling, you use happy words to write about ideas that are happy. When you use the writing trait of voice, you try to make the reader feel the way you do. Your writing voice replaces your speaking voice.

Which voice would you use to write about a low score you got on a report?

_____

4. Word Choice

You know that you can choose words to make your readers feel a certain way. **Word choice** is important in other ways, too. You must be sure the reader clearly understands what you are writing about. You should choose exact words to explain an idea. Words that appeal to the senses help readers draw a mental picture of your writing. The reader should be able to see, hear, taste, smell, and touch your ideas by reading your words. You should also choose strong action verbs to illustrate an idea. Did you see a <u>dog</u> or did you see a <u>fuzzy, white poodle</u>? Did the squirrel <u>go</u> up the tree or <u>scamper</u> up the tree?

Which words could you choose to write about that low score you got on your report?

_____

_____

WRITE AWAY

What are some words that you could use to describe a place you would like to live?

_____

_____

_____

_____

_____

© Harcourt Achieve Inc. All rights reserved.

The Seven Traits of Good Writing, page 3

5. Sentence Fluency

Sentence fluency is the way that you order words in your sentences. You want your words to flow smoothly. You want the writing to have a rhythm. You can gain sentence variety by changing the length of your sentences. You can also write sentences that have different patterns. Some sentences might begin with a noun. Others might begin with a preposition, an adjective, or an adverb. Read your sentences aloud. Do they flow or stumble?

Write a sentence that you think has good fluency. Read it aloud.

_____

6. Conventions

The **conventions** are all the rules of grammar and writing. Does each sentence have the correct end punctuation? Is each sentence complete? Do you have fragments or run-ons? Are the words spelled correctly? Do you have good subject-verb agreement? Is the meaning clear? Follow the rules to correct the mistakes in your writing.

7. Presentation

Presentation is the way your words and illustrations look on the page. Your work should be neat and clean. It should be easy to read. The illustrations should show the most important ideas. And don't forget a good title! A good title makes readers want to read your writing.

Would you want to read a book titled <u>Secret Things</u>? Why or why not?

_____

_____

You will use these writing traits all through the writing process. You do want to do your best work. You can use the Writing Traits Checklist on pages 117 and 118 to help you become a better writer.

WRITE AWAY

Write a list of ten new titles for stories, songs, books, or movies. The titles should make a person want to experience the works.

_____   _____

_____   _____

_____   _____

_____   _____

_____   _____

Basic Rules of Writing

When you write, you can let your imagination run wild. You can write about your most personal feelings or create fantasy lands. As a writer, you can change the way you express yourself. You never stop learning how to write. Here are a few basic rules to make you a better writer.

Write What You Know
What kinds of things do you know a lot about? Write about things that interest you, if possible. You will write better if you understand and feel strongly about your topic.

What do you know a lot about? Make a list of topics you could write about.

_____

_____

_____

Stick to the Topic
Once you choose a topic, you must keep your writing focused on that topic. Remember, you want the audience to know what you're writing about. One way to stick to the topic is to organize. Make an outline of what you want to write. You can write an outline on paper or create one in your mind. You should have a good idea what you want to write before you begin to write. Otherwise, you won't get far.

If you were writing about rivers in Europe, would it be a good idea to include information about the Colorado River? Why or why not?

_____

_____

Drafts
After you organize, you are ready to write the first draft. Don't worry about mistakes or neatness in the first draft. The important thing is to put your ideas on paper. You can organize them better in later drafts. You can add or remove details later. You can correct errors later, too. Really, though, it's easier to organize before you write than to try to fix weak writing later. So, prewrite!

Reread and Edit
To be a good writer, you don't have to spell perfectly or know all the rules of grammar. But you should correct as many errors as you can. Read your work over and over until you have fixed your mistakes. Try reading your work aloud. That way, both your eyes and your ears can help you catch problems. Use the Proofreading Checklist on page 119 to help you find errors. When you have corrected as many problems as you can, you are ready to write your final draft.

WRITE AWAY

What are the strengths and weaknesses of your writing? What are some ways you can improve your writing?

_____

_____

_____

What Is a Sentence?

The **sentence** is one of the basic units of writing. A sentence is a group of words that expresses a complete thought. It begins with a capital letter and ends with a punctuation mark. A sentence has two main parts, a **subject** and a **predicate.**

- The subject tells who or what the sentence is about.
- The **complete subject** is all the words in the subject.

     The black dog chased the white cat around the house.

- The predicate tells what the subject is or does.
- The **complete predicate** is all the words in the predicate.

     The black dog **chased the white cat around the house.**

Are the words below sentences? Write *yes* or *no*.

_____ **1.** A new movie at the theater.

_____ **2.** A light mist is falling tonight.

_____ **3.** Two dogs fighting in the alley.

_____ **4.** From which country?

_____ **5.** Doing his homework.

_____ **6.** A long time ago in a faraway land.

Write a word or words on the line to make each sentence complete.

7. A _____ rolled down the road.

8. _____ discovered some strange fossils.

9. The two gray horses _____.

10. A hot-air balloon _____.

11. The basketball coach _____.

12. _____ opened in the mall.

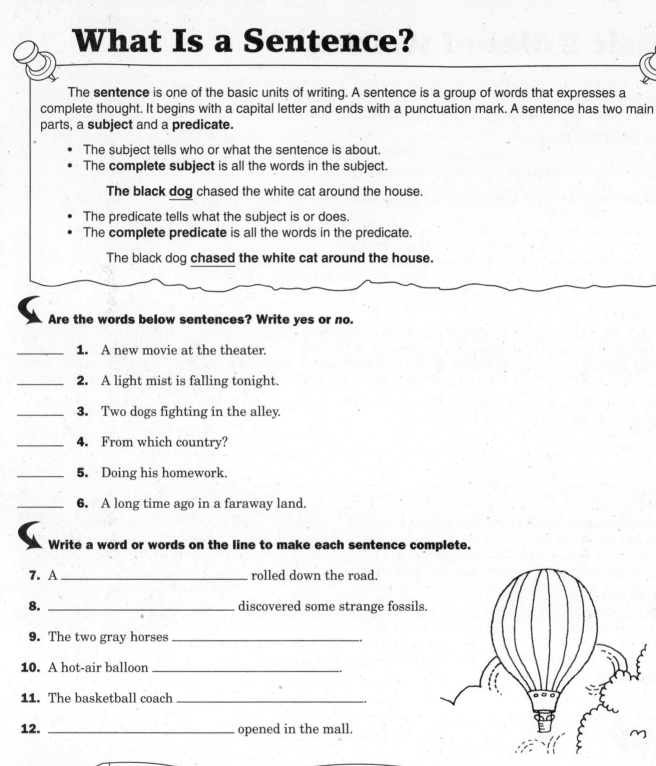

W R I T E   A W A Y

On another sheet of paper, write 12 short sentences like those just above. Include a subject or a predicate and a line for the other part. Trade with a friend or family member. Complete each other's sentences.

The Main Idea of a Sentence

A simple subject and a simple predicate form the **main idea** of a sentence. The simple subject and the simple predicate can stand alone as a complete sentence.

- The **simple subject** is the main noun or pronoun in the complete subject.
- The **simple predicate** is the main verb in the complete predicate.

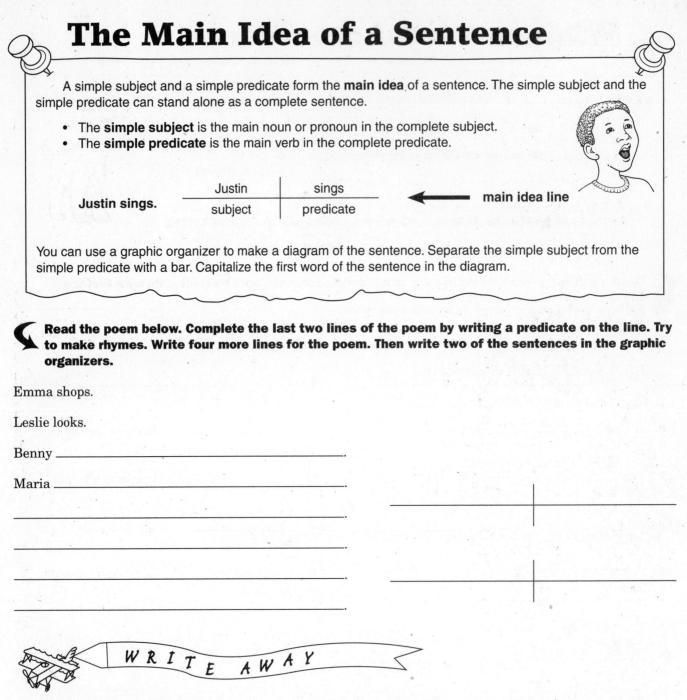

Justin sings.

Justin	sings
subject	predicate

← **main idea line**

You can use a graphic organizer to make a diagram of the sentence. Separate the simple subject from the simple predicate with a bar. Capitalize the first word of the sentence in the diagram.

Read the poem below. Complete the last two lines of the poem by writing a predicate on the line. Try to make rhymes. Write four more lines for the poem. Then write two of the sentences in the graphic organizers.

Emma shops.

Leslie looks.

Benny _____.

Maria _____.

_____

_____

_____

_____

W R I T E   A W A Y

On another sheet of paper, write a poem about the things people do. Then write each sentence in a graphic organizer that you draw.

© Harcourt Achieve Inc. All rights reserved.

Subject-Verb Agreement

The present tense verb you use as the simple predicate in a sentence must agree in number with the simple subject.

- Use a **singular verb** when the simple subject is singular.

    A **dog howls** in the distance. ◄───── a singular verb for a singular subject

- Use a **plural verb** when the simple subject is plural.

    Dogs howl in the distance. ◄───── a plural verb for a plural subject

Write a subject or present tense verb as needed to complete each sentence. Be sure that the subject and verb agree in number.

1. A bear _____ in the woods.

2. Thunder _____ in the valley.

3. The moon _____ in the night.

4. Seven horses _____ around the arena.

5. A _____ tastes sour.

6. _____ burn on the horizon.

7. Soft _____ blow through the treetops.

8. _____ laughs at the joke.

9. Flowers _____ in the springtime.

10. A student _____ his homework.

11. Two hikers on the trail _____ for help.

12. A red hawk _____ over the open field.

W R I T E   A W A Y

Here's a challenge. Some nouns can be both singular and plural. One example is the word *deer*. How many others do you know? Write a list on another sheet of paper. Then use each in a sentence.

Direct Objects

The main idea of your sentence may include a **direct object.** A direct object follows an action verb. It receives the action of the verb. The verb "takes" an object. The direct object is part of the complete predicate. It will be a noun or a pronoun.

Justin sings **songs.**

Justin	sings	songs
subject	verb	direct object

←—— **main idea line**

With a graphic organizer, you can easily see the main idea of the sentence. A long bar separates the simple subject from the simple predicate. A shorter bar separates the simple predicate from the direct object.

Write a direct object to complete each sentence. Then write two of the sentences in the graphic organizers below. Be sure to write the subject, predicate, and object in the correct place.

1. Birds eat _____.

2. My uncle found _____.

3. Barry called _____.

4. Students study _____.

5. Grandpa planted _____.

6. His sister writes _____.

7. The hurricane struck _____.

8. Trisha baked a _____.

9. Wesley wants _____.

10. Seven sisters seek _____.

WRITE AWAY

On another sheet of paper, write ten sentences that contain direct objects. Circle the object in each sentence. Then write each sentence in a graphic organizer that you draw.

© Harcourt Achieve Inc. All rights reserved.

Name _____   Date _____

Helping Verbs

Sometimes a main verb is lazy. It needs a helper to show action and time. A **helping verb** comes before the main verb in a sentence. The main verb and its helpers form a **verb phrase.** The last verb in a verb phrase is the main verb. Some common helping verbs are *am, is, are, was, were, will, must, can, may, have,* and *do.*

                    helping verbs   main verb
Our team **should have won.**

                    verb phrase

The subject and verb phrase form the main idea of the sentence. The main idea may include a direct object.

Mike	can build	houses

Mike **can build** houses.

✎ **Write a helping verb on the line to complete each sentence. Then, write the first and last sentences on the graphic organizers below.**

1. They _____ stopped.

2. Tina _____ organizing a party.

3. We _____ studying a boring subject in history.

4. I _____ never complete this assignment.

5. He _____ asking about you yesterday.

6. You _____ called me.

_____|_____|_____   _____|_____|_____

WRITE AWAY

On another sheet of paper, write ten sentences that contain helping verbs. Include direct objects in some of your sentences. Then draw ten graphic organizers and write your sentences in the organizers. Be sure to write each part in the correct place.

www.harcourtschoolsupply.com
© Harcourt Achieve Inc. All rights reserved.

Unit 2: Building Sentences
Core Skills Writing 8, SV 9781419099014

Linking Verbs

You can probably guess what a **linking verb** does. If you said that it links, you're right. A linking verb links the subject to a noun or an adjective in the complete predicate. The noun renames the subject, or the adjective describes the subject. Some linking verbs are *is, are, was, were, am,* and *been*. Some linking verbs can also be action verbs. These include *feel, look, seem, smell,* and *taste*.

- If the verb links the subject to a noun or pronoun, that noun or pronoun is called a **predicate nominative.**

    They **are neighbors.** ⬅━━ (predicate nominative)

- If the verb links the subject to an adjective, that adjective is called a **predicate adjective.**

    Phil **feels ill.** ⬅━━ (predicate adjective)

The predicate nominative and predicate adjective are part of the main idea of the sentence. When you write them in a graphic organizer, they go in the same place as the direct object. But the short bar leans back toward the subject. This leaning bar shows that the predicate nominative or predicate adjective is linked to the subject.

| They | are | \ neighbors | | Phil | feels | \ ill |

➤ **Write a linking verb to complete each sentence. Then write the sentence on the graphic organizer.**

1. I _____ exhausted.

2. Kara _____ confused.

3. Grackles _____ birds.

4. Slime _____ yucky.

W R I T E   A W A Y

On another sheet of paper, write ten short sentences that contain linking verbs. Include a predicate nominative or predicate adjective in each sentence. Then draw ten graphic organizers and write your sentences in the organizers.

Predicate Nominatives and Predicate Adjectives

You know that a linking verb links the subject to a noun, a pronoun, or an adjective in the complete predicate.

- If the verb links the subject to a noun or pronoun, that noun or pronoun is called a predicate nominative. Predicate nominatives can be common or proper nouns.

    My uncles are **carpenters.**   My favorite state is **Hawaii.**

- When the predicate nominative is a pronoun, you must use a subject pronoun.

    Who is the first contestant?   The first contestant is **I.**

- If the verb links the subject to an adjective, that adjective is called a predicate adjective. Predicate adjectives can be common or proper adjectives.

    Jacob is **smart.**   Diego is **Mexican.**

Write a predicate nominative noun to complete each sentence.

1. The man in the big hat is a _____.

2. John Wayne was a movie _____.

3. J. K. Rowling is a famous _____.

4. My favorite city is _____.

5. A jack-o-lantern is a Halloween _____.

Write a predicate nominative pronoun to complete each sentence. Be sure to use a subject pronoun.

6. The most talented singer was _____.

7. My best friend is _____.

8. _____ is your favorite actor?

Write a predicate adjective to complete each sentence.

9. The math test was _____.

10. Marci's new house is _____.

11. This velvet fabric feels _____.

12. The food smells and tastes _____.

Review: The Main Idea of a Sentence

If you can see—not read but see—your writing, you have a better idea of each part's role in the sentence. You can see the main idea of the sentence and the location of details. Seeing your writing can help you organize it better. Then you can build better sentences.

The main idea of a sentence is the most important part of the sentence. It tells the most important information in the sentence.

- The main idea may include only a simple subject and a simple predicate.   **Harrison helps.**
- The main idea may include a simple subject, a verb phrase, and a direct object.   **Harrison can help the homeless.**
- The main idea can include a simple subject, a simple linking verb, and a linked noun, pronoun, or adjective.   **Harrison is a volunteer.   He seems satisfied.**

Remember where each part of the sentence belongs in the graphic organizer.

| subject | verb | object | | subject | linking verb | pred. nom. or pred. adj. | ← main idea line |

Write a sentence that will fit each graphic organizer below. Write your sentence on the organizer. Then write your sentence on the line.

1. _____|_____

   _____

2. _____|_____|_____

   _____

3. _____|_____

   _____

4. _____|_____

   _____

© Harcourt Achieve Inc. All rights reserved.

Name _____   Date _____

Adding Details to Sentences

The main idea tells the most important part of a sentence. But you may want to include more information in your sentence. You can add **details** that tell more about the main idea. Details can tell whose, which, when, where, and how. Good details make your sentence more interesting.

A hungry horse ate **the fresh** hay.

You can see the main idea of the sentence in the graphic organizer below. All the parts of the main idea go above the main idea line. All the details go below the line. *A, hungry, the,* and *fresh* are adjectives that modify nouns in the sentence. Place the adjectives under the words they modify.

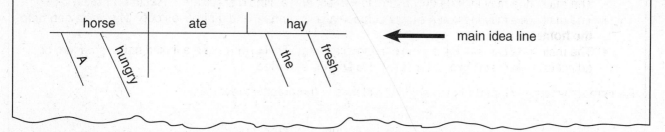

main idea line

Write details on the lines to complete each sentence. Then, on another sheet of paper, draw a graphic organizer for each sentence. Write each sentence on its organizer.

1. The _____ dog chewed the _____ bone.

2. A _____ actress wore a _____ hat.

3. A _____ boulder crushed a _____ truck.

4. The _____ man found a _____ treasure.

5. The _____ teacher discussed the _____ subject.

6. The _____, _____ water swamped the _____ boat.

7. _____ adults and _____ children saw a _____ creature.

8. The _____, _____ strawberries were _____.

WRITE AWAY

What was the best or worst thing that happened to you today? Write a few sentences about it. Use descriptive details in your sentences.

_____

_____

_____

_____

www.harcourtschoolsupply.com
© Harcourt Achieve Inc. All rights reserved.

Unit 2: Building Sentences
Core Skills Writing 8, SV 9781419099014

Expanding Sentences with Adjectives

How do you change a sad story into a happy story? All you have to do is change the adjective. **Adjectives** modify nouns and pronouns. Adjectives give details that help us tell one thing from another. With adjectives, we know the difference between a hot day and a cold day. Adjectives add spice to writing. But like most spices, you don't want to add too many. Choose your adjectives carefully.

- Look for sentences that do not express your ideas clearly.
- Think of adjectives that give a more exact image.

Blustery winter winds chilled **the five lost** hikers.

winds	chilled	hikers
Blustery winter		the five lost

Add adjectives to expand each sentence. Write your new sentence on the line. On another sheet of paper, draw a graphic organizer for each sentence. Write each sentence on its graphic organizer.

1. The store sells pastries.

_____

2. The girl baked cookies.

_____

3. The boy has hair.

_____

4. The man read a book.

_____

5. The guitarist played music.

_____

WRITE AWAY

On another sheet of paper, write adjectives that tell about each group listed below. See how many adjectives you can write for each group.

colors   tastes   sounds   shapes   textures   moods

Appeal to the Reader's Senses

Writing a good description is a special skill. You want your reader to see, smell, taste, hear, or feel as you do. To be a good descriptive writer, you must appeal to your reader's senses. Many adjectives appeal to these senses. But you must choose adjectives carefully to match your purpose and voice.

- **sight:** blue, short, straight, dark
- **smell:** smoky, dusty, rotten
- **taste:** sweet, bitter, sour, salty
- **touch:** warm, cool, rough, dull
- **hearing:** noisy, quiet, squeaky

Choose adjectives that you could use to describe each object. Write the adjectives on the line.

1. a watermelon _____

2. snow _____

3. cotton fabric _____

4. spaghetti _____

5. a firetruck _____

6. a park _____

7. a new coin _____

8. the first day of school _____

WRITE AWAY

On another sheet of paper, write adjectives that tell about each sense. How many adjectives can you write for each sense?

    sight   hearing   smell   touch   taste

Expanding Sentences with Adverbs

The difference between doing something and doing something <u>well</u> is just an adverb. Adverbs modify verbs, adjectives, or other adverbs. Most adverbs tell how, when, where, or to what extent. Many adverbs that tell how end in the letters *ly*.

The train rolled **slowly.**   (how)
He was here **yesterday.**   (when)
We saw bats **everywhere.**   (where)
The book was **very** scary.   (to what extent)

Adverbs are details that go under the main idea line in a graphic organizer. Write adverbs under the words they modify.

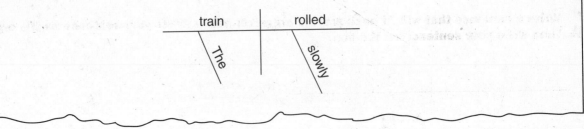

> **Write an adverb to expand each sentence. Then, on another sheet of paper, draw a graphic organizer for each sentence. Write each sentence on its organizer.**

1. Ice formed _____ .

2. The horse ran _____ .

3. The tired child slept _____ .

4. Mr. Crayton _____ caught the critter.

5. He _____ plays video games.

6. Wash your hands _____ .

7. _____ the river rose.

8. The driver turned _____ .

W R I T E   A W A Y

Most adverbs can be placed almost anywhere in a sentence. However, you should read your sentence aloud to hear which way sounds best. On another sheet of paper, write the adverb in parentheses in different places within the sentence. Read the sentences aloud. Which sounds best?

The time passed.   (slowly)

Review: Modifiers

Remember, when you see your writing, you have a better idea of each part's role in the sentence. You can see the main idea of the sentence and the location of details. Seeing your writing can help you organize it better. Then you can build better sentences.

You can add details to a sentence by using modifiers such as adjectives and adverbs.

- An adjective modifies a noun or a pronoun.   **black** truck
- An adverb modifies a verb, an adjective, or another adverb.

    dances **energetically**   **really** wrong   **very** smoothly

Modifiers are written under the main idea line in a graphic organizer. Write modifiers under the words they modify.

Write a sentence that will fit each graphic organizer below. Write your sentence on the organizer. Then write your sentence on the line.

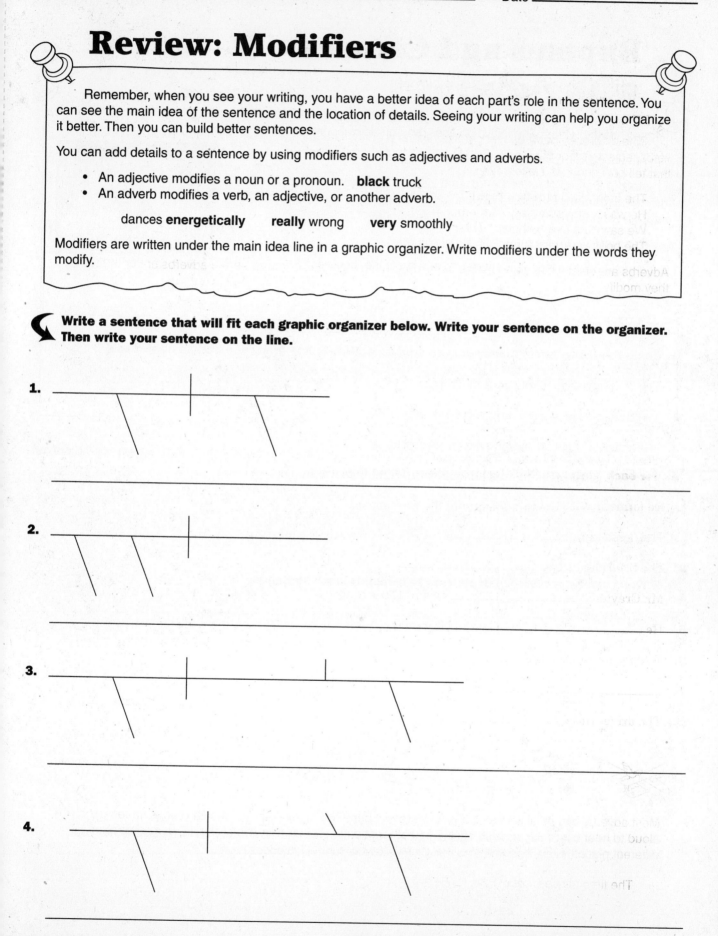

1.

_____

2.

_____

3.

_____

4.

_____

© Harcourt Achieve Inc. All rights reserved.
Unit 2: Building Sentences
Core Skills Writing 8, SV 9781419099014

Phrases and Clauses

A **phrase** is a group of words that does not have a subject or a predicate. Phrases are not complete sentences. They do not tell a complete thought. There are several kinds of phrases, such as prepositional phrases, gerund phrases, infinitive phrases, and participial phrases.

    into the cave   (prepositional phase)

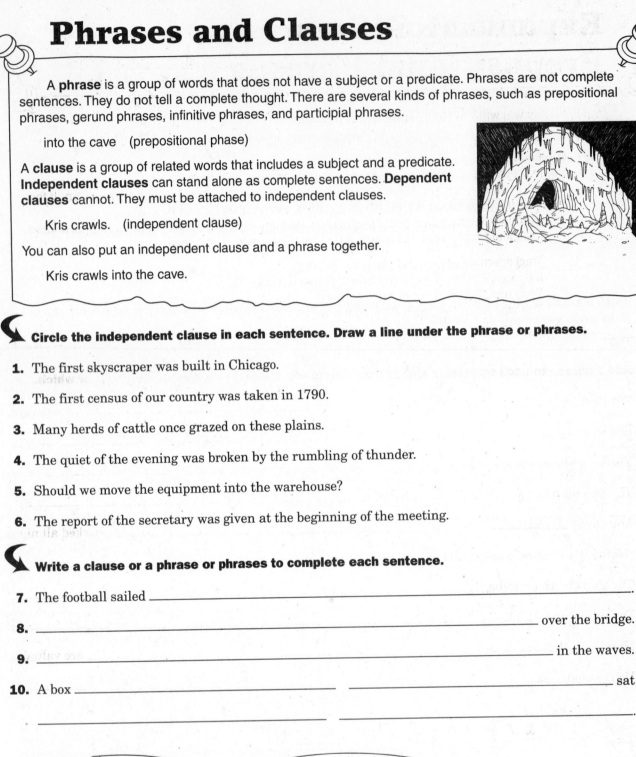

A **clause** is a group of related words that includes a subject and a predicate. **Independent clauses** can stand alone as complete sentences. **Dependent clauses** cannot. They must be attached to independent clauses.

    Kris crawls.   (independent clause)

You can also put an independent clause and a phrase together.

    Kris crawls into the cave.

Circle the independent clause in each sentence. Draw a line under the phrase or phrases.

1. The first skyscraper was built in Chicago.

2. The first census of our country was taken in 1790.

3. Many herds of cattle once grazed on these plains.

4. The quiet of the evening was broken by the rumbling of thunder.

5. Should we move the equipment into the warehouse?

6. The report of the secretary was given at the beginning of the meeting.

Write a clause or a phrase or phrases to complete each sentence.

7. The football sailed _____.

8. _____ over the bridge.

9. _____ in the waves.

10. A box _____ _____ sat

_____ _____.

_W R I T E   A W A Y_

On another sheet of paper, write 12 short independent clauses and 12 short phrases. Then cut them out. Mix and match the clauses and phrases. Can you make funny sentences?

© Harcourt Achieve Inc. All rights reserved.

Expanding Sentences with Prepositional Phrases

Many phrases you write will be **prepositional phrases.**

- Remember, a preposition shows the relation of a noun or pronoun to another word in a sentence.
- Some prepositions are *of*, *at*, *in*, *on*, *to*, *up*, *with*, *into*, *by*, and *from*.
- The noun or pronoun that follows the preposition is called the **object of the preposition.** If the object of the preposition is a pronoun, you must use an object pronoun.
- The preposition, the object of the preposition, and any other words form a prepositional phrase.
- Prepositional phrases can tell where, when, why, how, whose, or which.

  Traci spent the day **at the library.**   (where)
  My mother made the call **at once.**   (when or how)
  They are old friends **of mine.**   (whose)
  The woman **in the red hat** found the wallet.   (which)

Add a phrase to each sentence. Your phrase should tell where, when, whose, why, how, or which.

1. We found pecans _____

2. She went _____

3. The boys played basketball _____

4. The ground was covered _____

5. The puppy _____ barked all night.

6. George Washington was president _____

7. The ship struck an iceberg _____

8. The birds sang _____

9. Most _____ are valuable.

10. Don't stand _____

W R I T E   A W A Y

On another sheet of paper, write 15 prepositional phrases that tell where two chickens could hide in your house.   (in your sock drawer)

37

Adverb Phrases and Adjective Phrases

Prepositional phrases can tell where, when, why, or how. These kinds of prepositional phrases usually modify the predicate. They are known as **adverb phrases.** On a graphic organizer, each would be written under the verb.

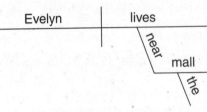

Prepositional phrases can also be used to tell which or whose. These kinds of prepositional phrases usually modify the subject, object, or predicative nominative. They are known as **adjective phrases.** On a graphic organizer, the phrase would be written under the subject, object, or predicate nominative.

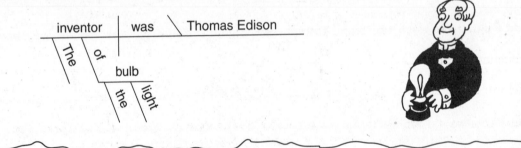

Write a sentence with a prepositional phrase. Look at the word in parentheses to tell what kind of prepositional phrase to write.

1. (when) _____

2. (whose) _____

3. (where) _____

4. (why) _____

5. (how) _____

6. (which) _____

7. (where) _____

8. (when) _____

W R I T E   A W A Y

On another sheet of paper, draw a graphic organizer for each of the sentences above. Write the sentence on the graphic organizer.

© Harcourt Achieve Inc. All rights reserved.

Gerunds and Gerund Phrases

A **verbal** is a verb form used as another part of speech. A gerund is a verbal. A **gerund** is a verb that ends in *ing* and functions as a noun. The gerund names an action. A gerund can take an object. Because gerunds function as nouns, they have many uses. Gerunds can be the subject of a sentence, the direct object, and the object of a preposition.

Prewriting is an important writing skill.

A gerund phrase includes the gerund, its object, and the object's modifiers.

Keeping his temper is hard for Jason.

Gerunds are not regular nouns, so they have a different form in the graphic organizer, too. In this sample, the subject is a gerund phrase.

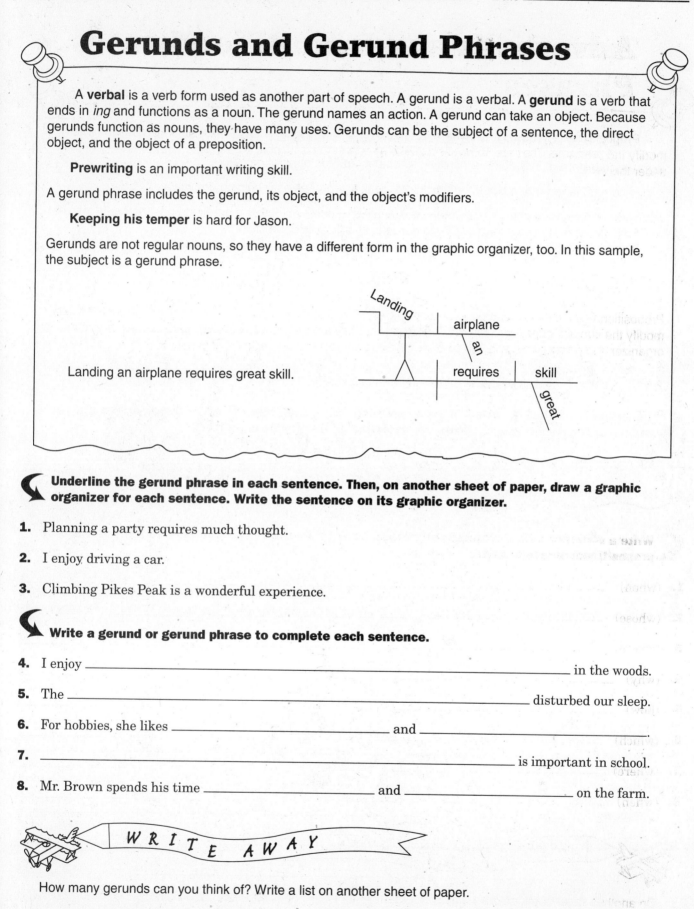

Landing an airplane requires great skill.

> Underline the gerund phrase in each sentence. Then, on another sheet of paper, draw a graphic organizer for each sentence. Write the sentence on its graphic organizer.

1. Planning a party requires much thought.

2. I enjoy driving a car.

3. Climbing Pikes Peak is a wonderful experience.

> Write a gerund or gerund phrase to complete each sentence.

4. I enjoy _____ in the woods.

5. The _____ disturbed our sleep.

6. For hobbies, she likes _____ and _____.

7. _____ is important in school.

8. Mr. Brown spends his time _____ and _____ on the farm.

W R I T E   A W A Y

How many gerunds can you think of? Write a list on another sheet of paper.

Name _____ Date _____

Infinitives and Infinitive Phrases

An infinitive is another kind of verbal. An **infinitive** is a verb that functions as a noun or adjective. The word *to* precedes the verb in an infinitive.

Many people like **to read.** ⬅——— infinitive as direct object

An **infinitive phrase** includes the infinitive, its object, and the object's modifiers.

My dream is **to write a book.** ⬅——— infinitive phrase as predicate nominative

Infinitives and infinitive phrases can serve as a subject, a direct object, or a predicate nominative. Infinitives and infinitive phrases use a form similar to gerunds in a graphic organizer.

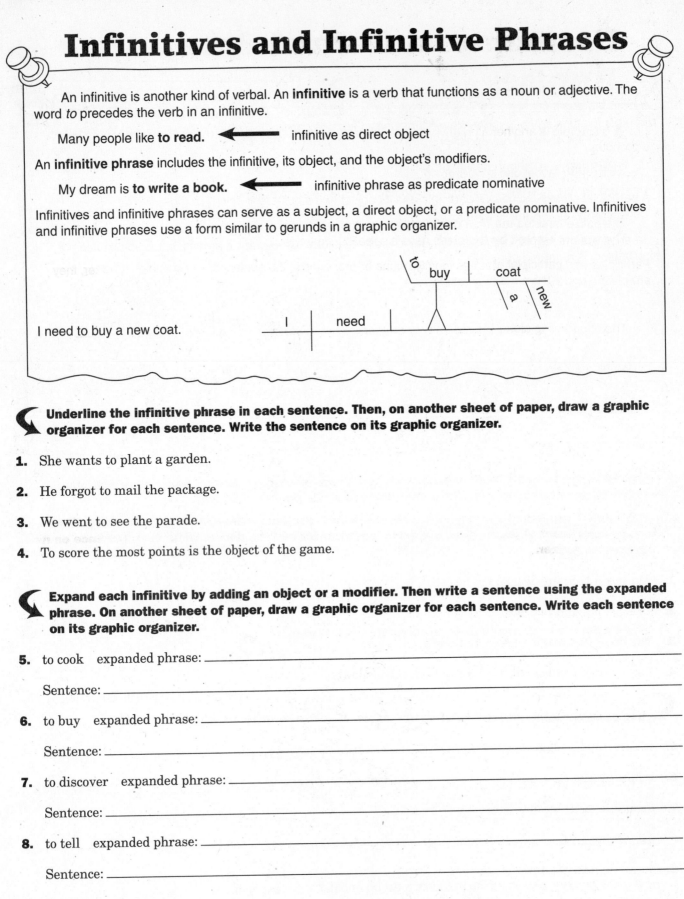

I need to buy a new coat.

Underline the infinitive phrase in each sentence. Then, on another sheet of paper, draw a graphic organizer for each sentence. Write the sentence on its graphic organizer.

1. She wants to plant a garden.

2. He forgot to mail the package.

3. We went to see the parade.

4. To score the most points is the object of the game.

Expand each infinitive by adding an object or a modifier. Then write a sentence using the expanded phrase. On another sheet of paper, draw a graphic organizer for each sentence. Write each sentence on its graphic organizer.

5. to cook   expanded phrase: _____

   Sentence: _____

6. to buy   expanded phrase: _____

   Sentence: _____

7. to discover   expanded phrase: _____

   Sentence: _____

8. to tell   expanded phrase: _____

   Sentence: _____

www.harcourtschoolsupply.com
© Harcourt Achieve Inc. All rights reserved.

Unit 2: Building Sentences
Core Skills Writing 8, SV 9781419099014

Participles and Participial Phrases

A **participle** is another kind of verbal. It is a form of a verb used as an adjective to modify a noun or a pronoun.

A **dripping** faucet can be a problem.

A participial phrase includes a participle and its object and modifiers, if any.

The police arrested the man **driving the car.**   (present participle)
The student **elected by the class** gave a speech.   (past participle)

Participles and participial phrases modify nouns or pronouns in the sentence. In a graphic organizer, they are placed under the word they modify.

The dog running along the road bit my brother.

```
       dog  |  bit  |  brother
   The  \           \  my
         running
          \
          along
              road
               \
               the
```

Underline the participle or participial phrase in each sentence. Circle the word it modifies. Then, on another sheet of paper, draw a graphic organizer for each sentence. Write each sentence on its graphic organizer.

1. Jon saw a running deer in the forest.

2. The girl playing the flute is my sister.

3. The dedicated artist worked endlessly.

4. The truck, burdened with its heavy load, rolled slowly.

Use each participle or participial phrase as an adjective to write a sentence.

5. whispering _____

6. injured _____

7. thinking about her new job

_____

8. standing near the fence

_____

© Harcourt Achieve Inc. All rights reserved.

Indirect Objects

An **indirect object** is the noun or pronoun that tells to whom or for whom an action is done. To have an indirect object, a sentence must have a direct object. The indirect object is usually placed between the action verb and the direct object. If the indirect object is a pronoun, use an object pronoun.

```
indirect        direct
 object         object
```

Chad gave **me** his old **CDs.**

The indirect object can be changed to a prepositional phrase, which may follow the direct object. The preposition used to form such a phrase is *to* or *for*. In a graphic organizer, the indirect object is placed under the verb.

Chad gave his old CDs to me.

> ➤ **Circle the indirect object in each sentence. Underline the direct object.**

1. I offered him a sandwich.

2. The nurse gave Sara the prescription.

3. Mike, did you sell Jim your truck?

4. Who sent Diego that long letter?

5. We gave the clerk our money.

> ➤ **Complete each sentence. Include an indirect object and a direct object. Then, on another sheet of paper, draw a graphic organizer for each sentence. Write each sentence on its graphic organizer.**

6. She gave _____ .

7. Have you found _____ ?

8. Please take _____ .

9. Mr. Gray sold _____ .

10. We have sent _____ .

W R I T E   A W A Y

On another sheet of paper, write five sentences that contain indirect objects. Then rewrite each sentence and change the indirect object to a prepositional phrase.

Expanding Sentences with Conjunctions

Remember, a **conjunction** is a connective. It joins words or groups of words. **Coordinate conjunctions** are one important kind of conjunction. A coordinate conjunction joins two words, two phrases, or two clauses of equal rank. Some coordinate conjunctions are *and*, *or*, *but*, *yet*, *for*, *then*, and *however*.

a lick **and** a promise   (*and* joins two nouns)
in the closet **or** by the fireplace   (*or* joins two prepositional phrases)
Gomer brought ice cream to eat; **however**, it melted in his lunch sack.
   (*however* joins two independent clauses)

Correlative conjunctions join pairs of ideas. Some correlative conjunctions are *either/or*, *neither/nor*, and *both/and*.

The movie was **not only** boring **but also** loud.

Underline the conjunction in each sentence. Write *coordinate* or *correlative* on the line to identify each conjunction.

_____ **1.** They left early, but they missed the bus.

_____ **2.** Both birds and mammals are warm-blooded.

_____ **3.** We have neither time nor money to waste.

_____ **4.** Did you see Willie or Max at the store?

Write sentences using coordinate conjunctions. Use a coordinate conjunction to join the kinds of words named in parentheses.

5. (nouns) _____

6. (adjectives) _____

7. (prepositional phrases) _____

_____

8. (independent clauses) _____

_____

W R I T E   A W A Y

Try to count the number of times you say or write the word *but* every day. On another sheet of paper, write a short story about what it would be like to live in a world that doesn't use this word.

Name _____ Date _____

Compound Subjects, Compound Predicates, and Compound Direct Objects

A **compound subject** has two or more simple subjects. The subjects are joined by a coordinate conjunction.

Terra *and* **I** often study math together.

A **compound predicate** has two or more simple predicates. The predicates are joined by a coordinate conjunction.

Ashley **ran, stumbled,** *and* **fell.**

My cousin **buys** *and* **remodels** old houses.

A **compound object** has two or more direct objects. The direct objects are joined by a coordinate conjunction.

I bought some **apples** *and* **oranges.**

When you write a compound subject, compound predicate, or direct object in a graphic organizer, you add the conjunction on a dotted line. The dotted line connects the two subjects or predicates.

Krystal and Kirk washed and dried the pots and pans.

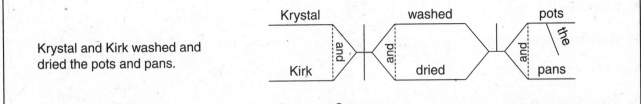

Write sentences with compound subjects, compound predicates, and compound objects as shown in parentheses. Then, on another sheet of paper, draw a graphic organizer for each sentence. Write the sentence on the graphic organizer.

1. (compound subjects) _____

2. (compound predicates with one direct object) _____

3. (compound predicates with compound direct objects) _____

_____

4. (compound subjects and compound predicates) _____

_____

WRITE AWAY

On another sheet of paper, write 12 compound subjects, 12 compound predicates, and 12 compound objects. Cut them out. Mix and match the parts. Write the sentences you made on a sheet of paper.

© Harcourt Achieve Inc. All rights reserved.

Agreement of Verbs and Compound Subjects

The subject of a sentence must agree in number with the verb. A singular subject must have a singular verb. A plural subject must have a plural verb.

- A compound subject that uses the word *and* is a plural subject. It requires a plural verb.

  Drawing **and** painting **are** good hobbies.

- A compound subject that uses the word *or* can be plural or singular. The verb agrees with the part of the compound subject closer to the verb.

  An orange **or** a banana **is** a healthy snack.
  Raisins **or** an apple **is** a healthy snack.
  A banana **or** carrots **are** a healthy snack.

➤ **Write a verb to complete each sentence. Be sure your verb agrees with the subject.**

1. Ernesto and Telli _____ in a local orchestra.

2. The musicians and the ushers _____ volunteers.

3. Todd, Terra, or Thomas _____ your ticket.

4. Museums, theaters, and libraries _____ found in many large cities.

5. A box of pens or a box of markers _____ in the desk.

6. Three dogs or a cat _____ on the farm.

➤ **Write a compound subject to complete each sentence. Be sure your subject agrees with the verb.**

7. A _____ or _____ are good to eat.

8. _____ or a _____ was in the box.

9. _____ and _____ make a good meal.

10. A _____ or a _____ is scheduled for the talent contest.

W R I T E   A W A Y

On another sheet of paper, write 12 sentences. Each sentence should have a compound subject and a compound predicate. Be sure your verbs agree with your compound subject. Both verbs will be either singular or plural.

Name _____ Date _____

Subordinate Conjunctions

Subordinate conjunctions are another important kind of conjunction. A subordinate conjunction joins two clauses of unequal rank. A subordinate conjunction joins a **dependent clause** to an **independent clause.** The independent clause has a higher rank than the dependent clause. The main idea of the sentence goes in the independent clause. Some subordinate conjunctions are *as, because, before, since, when, where,* and *that.*

      independent clause   dependent clause

    The movie started **before we found our seats.**

Because a dependent clause is less important than an independent clause, it goes below the main idea line in a graphic organizer.

We can leave when you are ready.

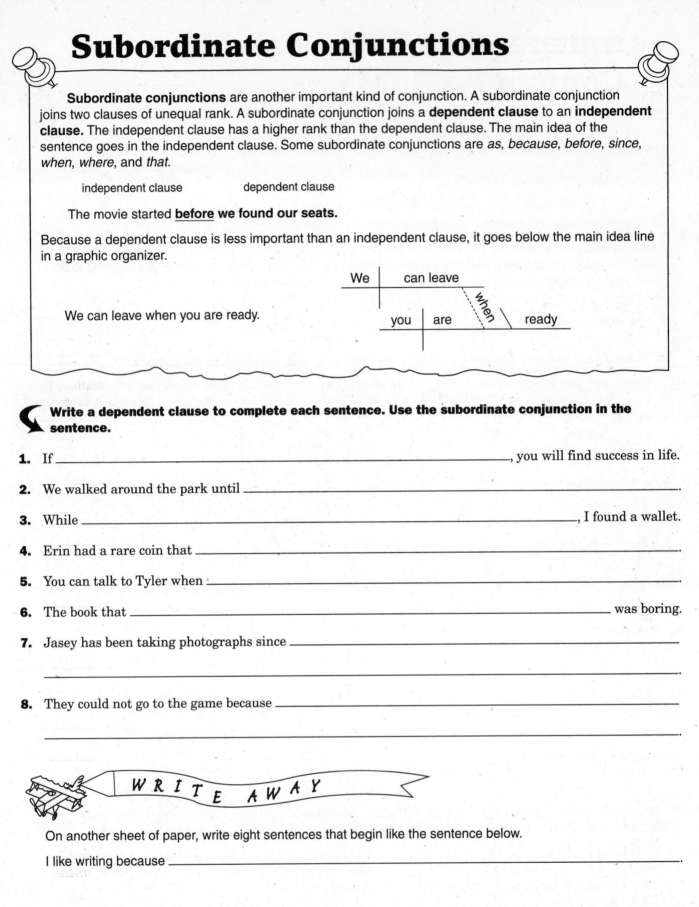

Write a dependent clause to complete each sentence. Use the subordinate conjunction in the sentence.

1. If _____, you will find success in life.

2. We walked around the park until _____.

3. While _____, I found a wallet.

4. Erin had a rare coin that _____.

5. You can talk to Tyler when _____.

6. The book that _____ was boring.

7. Jasey has been taking photographs since _____

    _____.

8. They could not go to the game because _____

    _____.

W R I T E   A W A Y

On another sheet of paper, write eight sentences that begin like the sentence below.

I like writing because _____.

© Harcourt Achieve Inc. All rights reserved.
Core Skills Writing 8, SV 9781419099014

Independent and Dependent Clauses

A subordinate conjunction joins two clauses of unequal rank. A subordinate conjunction joins a dependent clause to an independent clause. The main idea of the sentence goes in the independent clause. You must decide which information is more important. Then, write the more important information in the independent clause.

Ansel Adams started taking pictures. He was a teenager.
Ansel Adams started taking pictures **when** he was a teenager.

An independent clause tells a complete thought and can stand alone as a sentence. A dependent clause does not express a complete thought and cannot stand alone. A dependent clause must be attached to an independent clause. A dependent clause is also known as a **subordinate clause.**

She lost the ring. That you gave her.   (incorrect)
She lost the ring that you gave her.   (correct)

Read each set of sentences. Circle the sentence that contains the more important information. Then use the two sentences to write a new sentence. Use a subordinate conjunction to write a sentence containing an independent clause and a dependent clause. You can change some words if necessary.

1. The project was finished. Every girl did her share of the work.

_____

2. Photographing animals is difficult. They are unpredictable.

_____

3. Carla used a telephoto lens. She would not startle the hawk.

_____

4. You were at school. I bought groceries and cooked dinner.

_____

5. I prefer taking underwater pictures. The water makes photography more challenging.

_____

W R I T E   A W A Y

On another sheet of paper, rewrite the two sentences below as one sentence containing an independent clause and a dependent clause. Use these subordinate conjunctions: *because, since, when, before, where, after, although.* Which of your new sentences makes the most sense?

The night was cool. The walk was enjoyable.

Adjective Clauses and Adverb Clauses

An adjective clause is a dependent clause that modifies a noun or pronoun. It can tell which one or what kind. It usually modifies the word directly before it in the sentence. Most adjective clauses begin with a **relative pronoun.** A relative pronoun relates an adjective clause to the noun or pronoun the clause modifies. *Who, whom, whose, which,* and *that* are relative pronouns.

The hat **that she purchased** was on sale.

An adverb clause is a dependent clause that modifies a verb, an adjective, or another adverb. It can tell how, why, or under what condition. An adverb clause begins with a subordinate conjunction.

We arrived **before the store opened.**

In a graphic organizer, the adjective clause or adverb clause is written under the word it modifies.

```
hat    |    was            We  |  arrived
 The  that  on                    before
           sale
she    |  purchased         store  |  opened
                             the
```

Write an adjective clause or adverb clause to complete each sentence below. Then, on another sheet of paper, draw a graphic organizer for each sentence. Write each sentence on its graphic organizer.

1. The person who _____ won the election.

2. Always do the work that _____.

3. The band played in clubs that _____

4. The man whose _____ called the police.

5. The boat was gone when _____.

6. She overslept because _____.

7. We found the backpack where _____.

8. Since _____, I have not felt well.

9. They came home after _____

10. The bike that _____ had been stolen.

© Harcourt Achieve Inc. All rights reserved.
Unit 2: Building Sentences
Core Skills Writing 8, SV 9781419099014

Review: Connectives

Prepositions, conjunctions, and relative pronouns are connectives. They join parts of sentences.

- A preposition shows the relation of a noun or pronoun to another word in a sentence. Some prepositions are *of, at, in, on, to, up, by,* and *from.*
- The preposition, its object, and any other words make up a prepositional phrase.
- A coordinate conjunction connects words or groups of words of equal rank. Some coordinate conjunctions are *and, or, but,* and *yet.*
- A subordinate conjunction joins two clauses of unequal rank. Some subordinate conjunctions are *because, before, after, although,* and *that.*
- A relative pronoun joins an adverb clause to the independent clause. Some relative pronouns are *who, whom, whose, which,* and *that.*

A graphic organizer shows the role of connectives in the sentence.

Eva and Andrew cheered when their team scored.

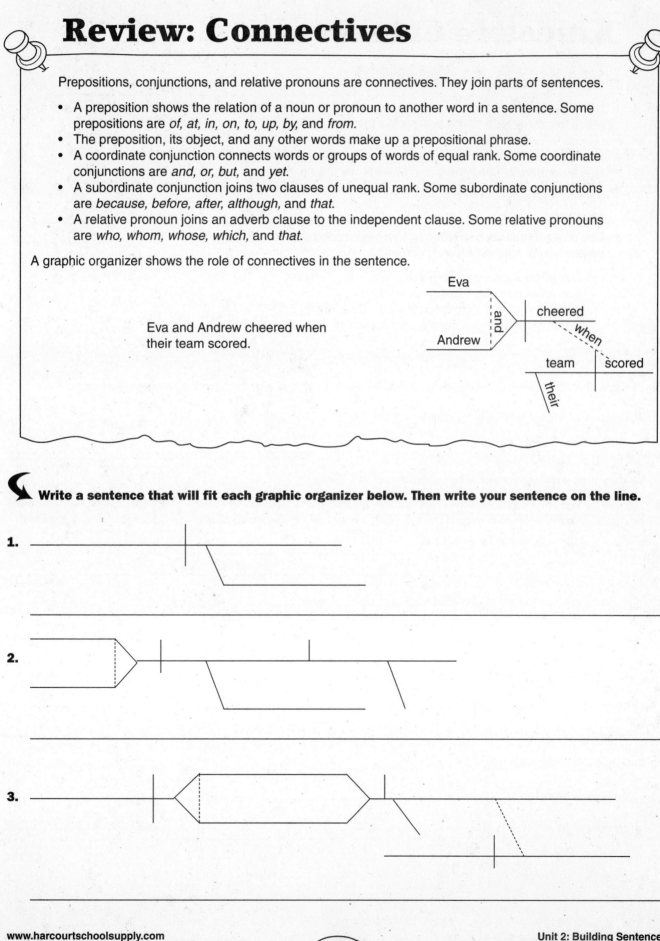

Write a sentence that will fit each graphic organizer below. Then write your sentence on the line.

1. _____

2. _____

3. _____

Name _____   Date _____

Kinds of Sentences

There are four basic kinds of sentences: declarative, interrogatory, imperative, and exclamatory.

- Use a **declarative sentence** to make a statement or give information. Begin a declarative sentence with a capital letter. End it with a **period (.)**.
- Use an **interrogative sentence** to ask a question or get information. Begin an interrogative sentence with a capital letter. End it with a **question mark (?)**.
- Use an **imperative sentence** to make a request or to give a command. Begin an imperative sentence with a capital letter. End it with a period or an **exclamation mark (!)**.
- The subject of an imperative sentence is the person to whom the request or command is given (*you*). The subject usually does not appear in the sentence. It is called an **understood subject**.
- Use an **exclamatory sentence** to show excitement or strong feeling. Begin an exclamatory sentence with a capital letter. End it with an exclamation mark.

    Mammals are warm-blooded animals.   (declarative)
    Are you a mammal?   (interrogative)
    (You) Go find me a mammal or two.   (imperative)
    Some mammals are creepy!   (exclamatory)

Follow the directions to write sentences. Be sure to begin and end each sentence correctly.

1. Write a declarative sentence about a river.

_____

2. Write an interrogative sentence about an event in history.

_____

3. Write an imperative sentence about doing homework.

_____

4. Write an exclamatory sentence about an erupting volcano.

_____

WRITE AWAY

On another sheet of paper, write five interrogative sentences. Write five declarative sentences to answer your questions. Then write five imperative sentences that give a command and five exclamatory sentences that respond to the commands.

www.harcourtschoolsupply.com
© Harcourt Achieve Inc. All rights reserved.

Unit 2: Building Sentences
Core Skills Writing 8, SV 9781419099014

End Punctuation

Be sure to use the correct punctuation at the end of your sentences.

- Use a **period (.)** at the end of a declarative sentence.
- Use a **question mark (?)** at the end of an interrogative sentence.
- Use a period or an **exclamation mark (!)** at the end of an imperative sentence.
- Use an exclamation mark at the end of an exclamatory sentence.

I wrote a poem about ghosts.   Would you like to hear it?
Be quiet so I can concentrate.   Your poem is spooky!

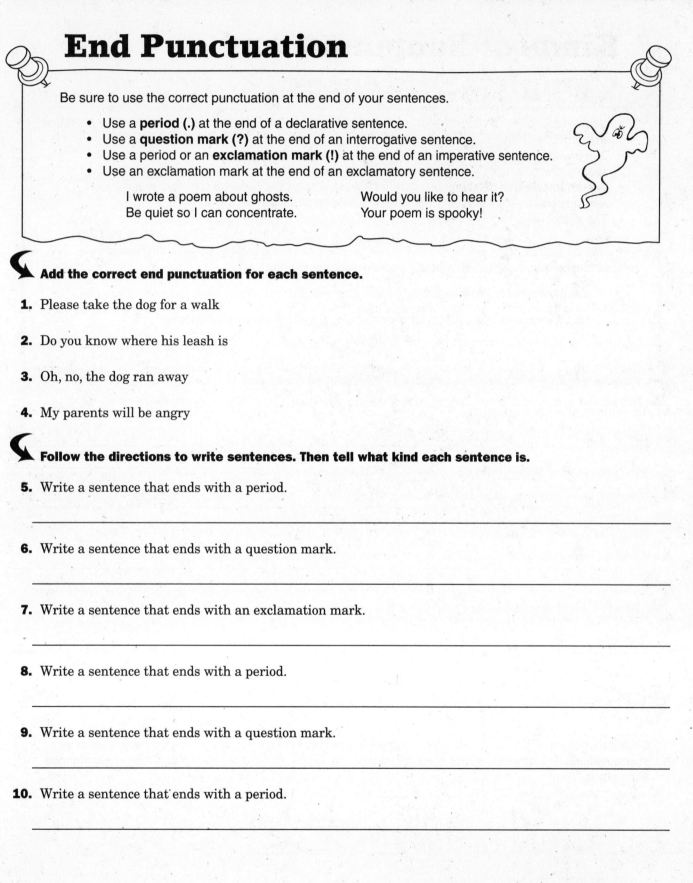

Add the correct end punctuation for each sentence.

1. Please take the dog for a walk

2. Do you know where his leash is

3. Oh, no, the dog ran away

4. My parents will be angry

Follow the directions to write sentences. Then tell what kind each sentence is.

5. Write a sentence that ends with a period.

_____

6. Write a sentence that ends with a question mark.

_____

7. Write a sentence that ends with an exclamation mark.

_____

8. Write a sentence that ends with a period.

_____

9. Write a sentence that ends with a question mark.

_____

10. Write a sentence that ends with a period.

_____

© Harcourt Achieve Inc. All rights reserved.   Core Skills Writing 8, SV 9781419099014

Simple, Compound, and Complex Sentences

- A **simple sentence** contains only one complete thought. It contains only one independent clause.

   Karlo was fishing for sharks in the pond.

- A **compound sentence** has two or more simple sentences. It has two or more complete thoughts. It contains two or more independent clauses.

- A **compound sentence** is joined by a coordinate conjunction such as *and, or,* or *but.* Use a **comma (,)** before a conjunction that joins two simple sentences.

   Karlo hooked a shark**, and** the shark pulled him into the water.

- A **complex sentence** contains one independent clause and one or more dependent clauses.

   Karlo was near the bottom of the pond before he knew what had happened.

Rewrite each simple sentence to make it a compound sentence.

1. The shark pulled Karlo deeper.

_____

2. Karlo saw a strange light ahead.

_____

3. Soon Karlo was in an underwater city.

_____

Rewrite each simple sentence to make it a complex sentence.

4. The shark released Karlo.

_____

5. Karlo could breathe underwater.

_____

6. Karlo could see the surface of the pond far above.

_____

WRITE AWAY

Write six simple sentences. Have a friend or family member write six simple sentences, too. Then exchange sentences. Rewrite each other's simple sentences to make them compound or complex sentences.

© Harcourt Achieve Inc. All rights reserved.

Using Commas

- Use a **comma** before the word *and, but,* or *or* when two sentences are joined in a compound sentence.

  The little man spoke to me, **but** I could not understand him.

- Use commas to separate three or more words in a **series**.

  Celia can speak **English, French, and Spanish.**

- Use a comma to separate an introductory word, name, phrase, or clause from the rest of the sentence.

  Jon, can you speak German?
  In my opinion, English is the hardest language to learn.

Complete each compound sentence by adding a second sentence. Be sure to add a comma and a conjunction.

1. Ava visited France last summer _____.

2. Later she rode the train to Germany _____.

3. She flew back to Texas on a plane _____.

Complete each sentence by adding a series of three or more words. Be sure to add commas and a conjunction.

4. I have packed _____ for the camping trip.

5. Near our campsite were _____.

6. _____ were in the woods.

Complete each sentence by adding an introductory word, phrase, or clause. Be sure to add a comma.

7. _____ a bear is chasing me!

8. _____ be sure to bring a tent.

W R I T E   A W A Y

Think about how you use commas when you write. Write a few sentences explaining how commas are useful to you.

_____

_____

© Harcourt Achieve Inc. All rights reserved.
53

Name _____   Date _____

Review: Working with Sentences

You can make your writing better by using different kinds of sentences.

➤ **Follow the directions to write sentences. Be sure to begin and end each sentence correctly.**

1. Write a simple declarative sentence about animals.

_____

2. Write a simple exclamatory sentence about your favorite singer.

_____

3. Write a simple interrogative sentence about a current event.

_____

4. Write a compound declarative sentence about a place you have visited.

_____

5. Write a compound imperative sentence about a job.

_____

6. Form a compound sentence by writing a second sentence. Be sure to add a comma and a conjunction.

A dim light flickered in the abandoned house _____

_____

7. Write a simple declarative sentence that contains a series.

_____

8. Write a complex sentence that uses the subordinate conjunction *because*.

_____

_____

9. Write a complex sentence that uses the subordinate conjunction *where*.

_____

_____

10. Write a complex sentence that uses the relative pronoun *that*.

_____

_____

© Harcourt Achieve Inc. All rights reserved.
Core Skills Writing 8, SV 9781419099014

Active and Passive Verbs

Strong verbs make writing livelier and more active. They keep your reader interested. Try this. Write a sentence and read it aloud. How does it sound? Does it make you fall asleep? If it does, it will make your reader fall asleep, too. Maybe you need stronger verbs. Let's test. What do you think of this sentence?

The winter air **has** made us very cold.

It is boring. The verb *was* is rather weak. *Was* is a **passive verb.** All of the *be* verbs (*is, are, was, were, am, be, been, being*) are passive. When you use a passive verb, the subject receives the action. When you use an **active verb,** the subject performs the action. The sentence needs an **active verb.**

The cold winter air **chilled** us to the bone.

Chilled is an active verb. We can see the action in our heads. We are more interested. To make your writing more interesting, use active verbs as much as possible.

Rewrite each sentence. Change the passive verbs to active verbs. You may have to change the way the sentence is written.

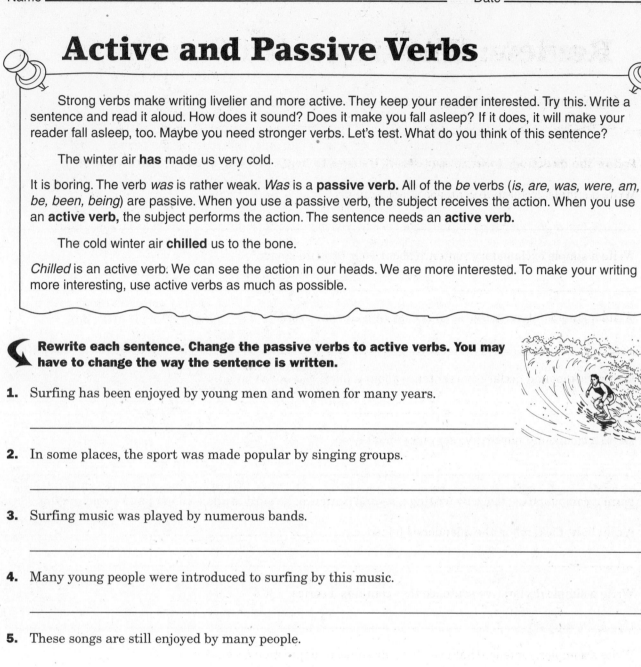

1. Surfing has been enjoyed by young men and women for many years.

   _____

2. In some places, the sport was made popular by singing groups.

   _____

3. Surfing music was played by numerous bands.

   _____

4. Many young people were introduced to surfing by this music.

   _____

5. These songs are still enjoyed by many people.

   _____

6. The waves are carefully watched by surfers all along the coast.

   _____

7. A sense of freedom is achieved by riding the waves.

   _____

8. This sense of freedom is what makes surfing so popular.

   _____

Verb Tense

Tense means "time." So, **verb tense** tells the time of the action or being.

- Use a **present tense verb** to tell what is happening now. The action is continuing.
- Use a **past tense verb** to tell what happened in the past. The action is completed.
- Use a **future tense verb** to tell what will happen in the future. The action has not yet begun.

We **walk** now.	We **walked** yesterday.	We **will walk** next week.
(present tense)	(past tense)	(future tense)

If you use the wrong verb tense, your reader will be lost in time. That's not good. So check your verbs. Be sure your verb tense tells when things are happening.

Rewrite each paragraph, correcting any sentences containing a verb that is not consistent with the rest of the paragraph. If there is a good reason for a shift in verb tense, explain it in writing.

1. The race was on. Carlos runs around the track as fast as he can. He lifted one foot and then the other. He runs and ran some more. Finally, he reached the finish line, and the race ends.

_____

_____

_____

2. I had never been camping before. I expect the activities to be hard and boring. What I don't expect was the beauty and peace of the woods. I enjoy every minute of the camping trip.

_____

_____

_____

3. My father's favorite game has always been dominoes. He likes dominoes because the game keeps his mind active. When he was young, he played dominoes when he was a soldier. He says that dominoes were the one thing that made the war bearable.

_____

_____

_____

WRITE AWAY

Write a list of 15 verbs on another sheet of paper. Then make a chart with three columns. At the top of one column, write *present tense.* At the top of the second column, write *past tense.* At the top of the third column, write *future tense.* Write your 15 verbs in the correct place in the chart. Complete the chart by writing the correct tense of each verb in the columns.

Writing Descriptive Sentences

When you write a descriptive sentence, you give the reader details. Use specific details that tell who, what, when, where, and how. Your descriptive sentence should let the reader "see" the scene in his or her mind. The following sentence tells about the object, but the reader cannot "see" the scene.

Mount Rushmore is impressive and awe-inspiring.

This sentence needs more specific adjectives than "impressive" and "awe-inspiring." Those adjectives really only tell what the writer thinks about the topic. They don't really describe the topic. Good descriptive sentences use strong verbs and specific adjectives and adverbs. Here's a better descriptive sentence.

The four huge granite faces carved into Mount Rushmore gaze peacefully into the distance.

Rewrite each sentence to make it more descriptive. Use strong verbs and specific adjectives or adverbs.

1. Clouds floated in the sky.

_____

2. A hawk patrolled the field.

_____

3. Animals moved through the grass.

_____

4. Leaves rustled in the breeze.

_____

5. Birds were singing through the valley.

_____

6. The sky was beginning to turn gray.

_____

7. Soon the night would be here.

_____

WRITE AWAY

What is your favorite season? On another sheet of paper, write ten descriptive sentences about it. Use strong verbs and specific adjectives or adverbs in your sentences.

Writing Descriptive
Sentences, page 2

Good description creates a mental picture for the readers. How do you create a mental picture? You use specific details. Adjectives are good for details. Adjectives can tell color, size, smell, feel—all the good senses. You want your words to control what your readers see in their minds. You must appeal to their senses. Think about your word choices. That's what good writers do.

The cold, sweet juice of the green and red melon tingled my tongue.

You want to describe your favorite place for someone. Think about your favorite place. Then, write five adjectives for each sense to describe that place. Remember, think about your choices.

Sight: _____

Sound: _____

Touch: _____

Smell: _____

Taste: _____

Choose the best adjective for each sense from your lists above. Use the five best adjectives to write a descriptive paragraph about your favorite place. Use another sheet of paper if necessary. Remember, create a mental picture for your reader. Don't just write sentences listing the adjectives.

Best adjectives: _____

_____

_____

_____

_____

_____

_____

W R I T E   A W A Y

Look outside a window. On another sheet of paper, write ten sentences to describe what you see. Try to appeal to all the senses.

Writing Descriptive Sentences, page 3

Strong adjectives are good for creating mental pictures. Adverbs are good, too. But strong verbs are better. Strong verbs can make your description livelier.

The winter wind **whistled** down the chimney.

Write five active verbs that mean the same as the words given. Write only verbs. Do not use adverbs.

1. hold with your hand _____

2. go _____

3. say _____

4. see _____

5. find _____

Revise each sentence. Use a strong verb. Use strong adjectives. Make your writing clear and direct.

6. A player on the team that was behind made a shot that went in the goal just when a buzzer went off that

meant that the game was over. _____

_____

7. The building was unusual.

_____

8. The man in charge of the team had another boy go in the game to pitch for the boy who was pitching when someone on the other team got a hit and drove in three runs.

_____

_____

9. The summer sunrise was beautiful.

_____

W R I T E   A W A Y

On another sheet of paper, rewrite the sentence below six times. Replace the verb with a stronger verb in each sentence.

The spelunker moved through the dim cave.

Name _____   Date _____

Using Figurative Language

Writers sometimes use **figurative language** to compare unlike things. The words in figurative language don't really mean what they say. If a man is very hot, he might say he feels like the sun. He doesn't really mean it, though. He is using figurative language.

- A **simile** compares two things by using *like* or *as*.
- A **metaphor** compares two things by speaking of one thing as if it were another. A metaphor does not use *like* or *as*.
- **Personification** makes nonhuman things seem human. Objects, ideas, places, or animals may be given human qualities. They may perform human actions.

The orchestra drums rumbled **like thunder.**   (simile)

The moon was **a silver ship sailing through a cloudy sea.**   (metaphor)

The **gentle breeze whispered good morning** to the new day.   (personification)

Complete each simile or metaphor.

1. Life is sometimes like _____.

2. Our emotions are like _____.

3. Time is _____.

4. The cool breeze was like _____.

5. The white clouds are _____.

Rewrite each sentence but use personification to make it more interesting.

6. A big fire burned the forest.

_____

7. The tree's branches moved in the wind.

_____

8. The sunshine was warm.

_____

W R I T E   A W A Y

Rewrite each sentence below on another sheet of paper. State the same idea, but use a simile, a metaphor, or personification.

My father works hard.
The desk was very heavy.
The sailboat moved across the waves.

© Harcourt Achieve Inc. All rights reserved.
Core Skills Writing 8, SV 9781419099014

Sentence Variety

Sentence variety makes your writing more interesting. Sentences that all begin the same way or have the same order are boring. There's a saying that "variety is the spice of life." Well, variety is the spice of writing, too. Let's look at some ways to spice up your writing.

- You can begin a sentence with an adjective or adverb.

    Thrilling were the patriotic music and fireworks at the celebration.
    Slowly the truck crossed the bridge and disappeared.

- You can begin a sentence with a preposition or the object of the sentence.

    At the lake we caught some fish.
    Some situations I try to avoid.

- You can change the order of the subject and the verb. This is called **inverted order.**

    Traveling in Europe **was** Eva's **wish.**
    Across the field **ran five deer.**

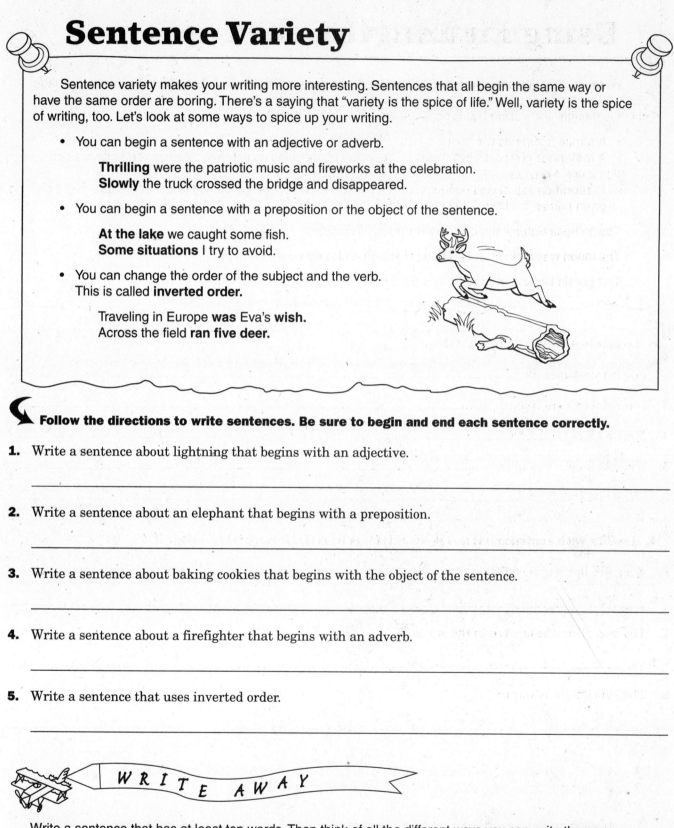

▸ **Follow the directions to write sentences. Be sure to begin and end each sentence correctly.**

1. Write a sentence about lightning that begins with an adjective.

_____

2. Write a sentence about an elephant that begins with a preposition.

_____

3. Write a sentence about baking cookies that begins with the object of the sentence.

_____

4. Write a sentence about a firefighter that begins with an adverb.

_____

5. Write a sentence that uses inverted order.

_____

W R I T E   A W A Y

Write a sentence that has at least ten words. Then think of all the different ways you can write the same thing. How many different ways can you begin the sentence? On another sheet of paper, write your sentence at least six different ways.

Original sentence: _____

Sentence Lengths

You can also get variety by changing the lengths of the sentences you write.

- Short sentences tell about the main idea or present actions better.

    The **lightning flashed** again and again.
    The **bear charged** at the hiker.

- Longer sentences help to explain details better.

    The **yellow** car **owned by the singer** sat **abandoned in the dark tunnel.**

- Compound sentences let you tell about two related ideas.

    My sister likes cats, but I prefer dogs.

- Complex sentences let you make one idea more important than another.

    After the sun went down, **we pitched our tents and built a campfire.**

Follow the directions to write sentences. Be sure to begin and end each sentence correctly.

1. Write a short sentence that shows a strong action.

_____

2. Write a longer sentence with several details.

_____

3. Write a longer compound sentence that tells about two related ideas.

_____

_____

4. Write a complex sentence that makes one idea more important than another idea.

_____

_____

W R I T E   A W A Y

On another sheet of paper, practice writing the same idea in sentences of different lengths. Do the shorter or longer sentences help you express yourself better? Explain why.

© Harcourt Achieve Inc. All rights reserved. Core Skills Writing 8, SV 9781419099014

Achieving Sentence Variety

You can achieve sentence variety by changing sentence lengths, sentence beginnings, or sentence types. You can add coordinate or subordinate conjunctions to expand sentences.

In this exercise, you are going to rewrite the following sentences. They are all short sentences. Remember, you want to have sentence variety. Follow the directions to write new sentences. Then write the sentences as a paragraph on another sheet of paper. Do you like the original version or your revised version better?

Pedro overslept. He missed the bus to school. He knew a shortcut. He decided to walk to school. He knew the shortcut was dangerous. He took the shortcut anyway. Along the way, Pedro fell off the path and broke his arm. The police came to rescue Pedro. Firefighters came to rescue him. After all the trouble he caused, Pedro decided to try to wake up on time.

1. The first two sentences are short and choppy. Combine the first two sentences with the subordinate conjunction *because*. Remember, you have to choose which information is more important. Put the less important information in the dependent clause.

_____

_____

2. The third and fourth sentences are short and choppy, too. Combine these two sentences with the subordinate conjunction *since*.

_____

_____

3. The fifth and sixth sentences are short and choppy. Combine these two sentences with a coordinate conjunction.

_____

_____

4. The seventh sentence is short, but it emphasizes the problem Pedro has. Let's leave it as is.

5. The eighth and ninth sentences are short and choppy. Combine these two sentences using a compound subject.

_____

_____

6. The tenth sentence is about the right length. Let's leave it as is.

Sentence Errors: Fragments

A good sentence expresses a complete idea. It has a subject and a predicate. It uses correct punctuation. But sentence errors can make your writing unclear and confusing. You need to check your writing to be sure you do not have sentence errors.

One common error is the **sentence fragment.** A sentence fragment is only a part of a sentence. It is not a complete sentence. It does not tell a complete thought. You should remove fragments from your writing.

Went on a trip to California.   (fragment—no subject)
Keesha's birthday next Friday.   (fragment—no predicate)
In the drawer by the sink.   (fragment—prepositional phrases)
Though he did all his homework.   (fragment—dependent clause)
She parked the car by the tall tree.   (complete sentence)

Rewrite each fragment to make it a complete sentence. If the group of words is a complete sentence already, write *not a fragment.*

1. Made a shot at the last minute.

_____

2. Cedric's shot won the big game.

_____

3. After Cedric made the shot.

_____

4. A reporter from the local TV station.

_____

5. Doing a report on local athletes.

_____

6. A college coach and a player from a pro team.

_____

7. Everyone happy after the game was over.

_____

8. Cedric was the hero for a day.

_____

Sentence Errors: Run-on Sentences

Another common error is the **run-on sentence**.

- A run-on sentence happens when you join two complete sentences without any punctuation. This error is also known as a **fused sentence**.
- To fix a run-on like this, join the two sentences with a comma and a coordinate conjunction.
- You can also use a period and write the run-on as two separate sentences.
- You can also separate the two independent clauses with a semicolon.
- You can also join the two sentences with a subordinate conjunction. You must make one idea more important than the other idea.

Your brain is an amazing organ you could not read without it.   (run-on)
Your brain is an amazing organ, **and** you could not read without it.   (fixed)
Your brain is an amazing organ. You could not read without it.   (fixed)
Your brain is an amazing organ; you could not read without it.   (fixed)
Because your brain is an amazing organ, you could not read without it.   (fixed)

Correct each run-on sentence. Write the new sentence or sentences on the line.

1. The brain is surrounded by three membranes the skull encloses the brain and these three membranes.

_____

_____

2. The brain reaches its full size by the time a person is twenty at that time, it weighs about three pounds.

_____

_____

3. The brain helps a person see, hear, touch, smell, and taste it also makes it possible for one to remember and forget, talk and write, and feel emotions.

_____

_____

_____

4. The brain has three main parts these parts are the cerebrum, the cerebellum, and the brain stem.

_____

_____

 W R I T E   A W A Y

Read sentence 2 aloud. Listen to your voice. Where does it tell you a period goes? Can reading your sentences aloud help? Write your ideas on another sheet of paper.

Sentence Errors: Run-on Sentences, page 2

- A run-on sentence also occurs when you join two complete sentences with only a comma. This error is also known as a **comma splice.**
- To fix a run-on like this, use a period and write the run-on sentence as two separate sentences.
- You can also join the two sentences with a comma and a coordinate conjunction.
- You can also separate the two independent clauses with a semicolon.
- You can also join the two sentences with a subordinate conjunction. You must make one idea more important than the other idea.

We went on a class trip to a water park, we had a lot of fun.   (run-on)
We went on a class trip to a water park. We had a lot of fun.   (fixed)
We went on a class trip to a water park, **and** we had a lot of fun.   (fixed)
We went on a class trip to a water park; we had a lot of fun.   (fixed)
When we went on a class trip to a water park, we had a lot of fun.   (fixed)

Correct each run-on sentence. Write the new sentence or sentences on the line.

1. The bus stopped in the parking lot, we all got off.

   _____

2. Jeremy ran ahead, the rest of us followed behind.

   _____

3. Sara did the water chute first, Jason went to the surf pond.

   _____

4. The sun was bright and warm, the water sparkled in the sunlight.

   _____

5. We sat at picnic tables for lunch, we ate sandwiches and fruit.

   _____

6. The day was over too soon, we did not want to go home.

   _____

WRITE AWAY

The comma splice was once called a comma blunder. What is a blunder? Which do you think is a better name for the error? Write your ideas on another sheet of paper.

Name _____ Date _____

Sentence Errors: Dangling Modifiers and Misplaced Modifiers

A modifier must be placed close to the word it modifies. A **dangling modifier,** or dangling participle, often has no word in the sentence to modify. The modifier is related to the first noun or pronoun that follows it.

Running to the window, a fire was seen.   (incorrect—The fire is not running.)
Running to the window, I saw a fire.   (correct—I am running.)

A **misplaced modifier** is positioned in the wrong place in the sentence. It must be placed near the word it modifies.

He **almost** spent fifty dollars.   (confusing—He was going to spend the money but didn't.)
He spent **almost** fifty dollars.   (clear—He spent nearly fifty dollars.)

Correct each dangling modifier by rewriting the sentence.

1. Entering the door, the front desk is seen.

_____

2. Walking down the avenue, the beautiful skyscraper was admired.

_____

3. Looking through the binoculars, the ship sank.

_____

4. Running down the road, my nose froze.

_____

5. Dangling by one leg from a pair of tweezers, the girl held the moth in front of her.

_____

Correct each misplaced modifier by rewriting the sentence.

6. They saw a man on a horse with a wooden leg.

_____

7. Jenna saw some shoes in a window that she liked.

_____

8. Serve one of the melons for lunch; keep the other melon for the picnic in the refrigerator.

_____

Building a Sentence

If you can see—not read but see—your writing, you have a better idea of each part's role in the sentence. You can see the main idea of the sentence and the location of details. Seeing your writing can help you organize it better. Use graphic organizers to diagram your sentences. Then you can build better sentences.

Writing is a process. Follow the steps to build a better sentence.

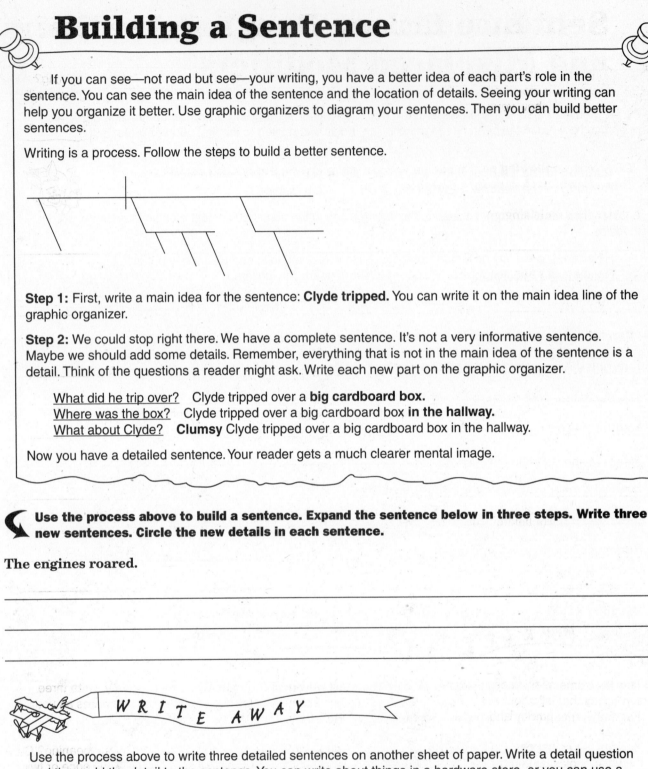

Step 1: First, write a main idea for the sentence: **Clyde tripped.** You can write it on the main idea line of the graphic organizer.

Step 2: We could stop right there. We have a complete sentence. It's not a very informative sentence. Maybe we should add some details. Remember, everything that is not in the main idea of the sentence is a detail. Think of the questions a reader might ask. Write each new part on the graphic organizer.

What did he trip over?   Clyde tripped over a **big cardboard box.**
Where was the box?   Clyde tripped over a big cardboard box **in the hallway.**
What about Clyde?   **Clumsy** Clyde tripped over a big cardboard box in the hallway.

Now you have a detailed sentence. Your reader gets a much clearer mental image.

Use the process above to build a sentence. Expand the sentence below in three steps. Write three new sentences. Circle the new details in each sentence.

The engines roared.

_____

_____

_____

W R I T E   A W A Y

Use the process above to write three detailed sentences on another sheet of paper. Write a detail question and then add the detail to the sentence. You can write about things in a hardware store, or you can use a topic of your choice. Then draw a graphic organizer for each sentence. Write each sentence on its organizer.

Self-Evaluation: What's Going On?

You've been studying hard, of course, and writing in many different ways. Have you learned anything? Do you think you are a better writer now? Do you know what a good sentence is? Well, on this page you will get a chance to show your stuff.

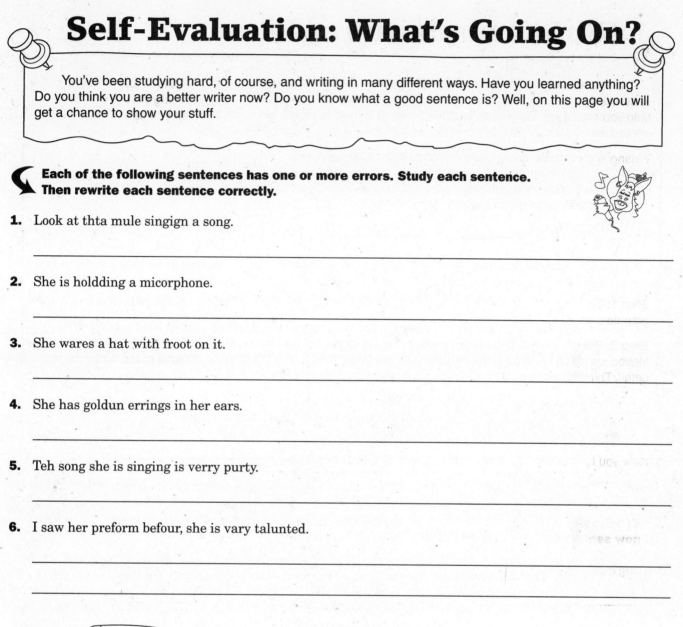

Each of the following sentences has one or more errors. Study each sentence. Then rewrite each sentence correctly.

1. Look at thta mule singign a song.

_____

2. She is holdding a micorphone.

_____

3. She wares a hat with froot on it.

_____

4. She has goldun errings in her ears.

_____

5. Teh song she is singing is verry purty.

_____

6. I saw her preform befour, she is vary talunted.

_____

_____

W R I T E   A W A Y

Take your time on this activity. You want to do your best writing. First, on another sheet of paper, write three sentences that tell about something you really like, such as music or a hobby. Look at the sentences as your first draft. Write quickly and get your ideas on paper. Be sure your main idea is strong and clear.

Revise your sentences. Do the sentences say what you mean? Will your reader understand your meaning? Can the word choice be improved? Think about your sentences for five minutes. Read each one aloud once or twice. Then, rewrite each sentence three more times. Read each sentence aloud as you are writing it. How does it sound? Is the punctuation correct? Add important details your reader will need to know.

Now choose the best version of each sentence. Write the three sentences in final form. Compare your final three sentences to the Self-Evaluation Checklist on page 121. Check each point that agrees with your writing. How good is your writing? On another sheet of paper, write three or four sentences that describe the style of your writing.

What Is a Paragraph?

A **paragraph** is a group of sentences that tells about one main idea. A good paragraph has unity, coherence, and emphasis. **Unity** means that every sentence in the paragraph supports the main idea. **Coherence** means that the parts of the paragraph have a logical order. **Emphasis** means that the important ideas are stressed, not minor or unnecessary ideas. A paragraph has three parts.

- The **topic sentence** tells the main idea of the paragraph.
- The **detail sentences** tell more about the main idea.
- The **concluding sentence** closes the paragraph. It restates the main idea and summarizes the information in the paragraph.

Read each paragraph below. How well does each paragraph tell about one main idea? Write a few sentences about each paragraph. Tell why it is or is not a good paragraph. Then, if you think the paragraph is weak, correct it and rewrite it on another sheet of paper.

1. All matter contains a positive or negative charge. Negative charges can move from one object to another. Static electricity results when an object gains or loses a charge. The objects may attract or repel each other. If they attract, they pull together. If they repel, they push apart. Objects with like charges repel each other, while those with opposite charges attract each other.

_____

_____

_____

_____

_____

2. In winter, food is hard to find in cold places. To avoid starving to death, some animals migrate. Others stay in the area. These animals first store up food in the form of body fat. I wonder if they hibernate. I wonder if they get really tired. Next, they find a safe place to spend the winter. Finally, they fall into a long, deep sleep. They sleep, or hibernate, through the cold winter and awake when the weather turns warmer. My brother sleeps all the time. Maybe he is hibernating. When an animal hibernates, its body temperature drops, and its heartbeat slows.

_____

_____

_____

_____

_____

What Is in a Paragraph?

A paragraph is a group of sentences about one main idea. The first sentence of the paragraph is **indented.** There are usually several sentences in a paragraph. Many paragraphs have five sentences. Try to avoid writing very long or very short paragraphs.

When you write a paragraph, you want it to have a logical order. A good paragraph has a certain movement. The information in the paragraph goes from

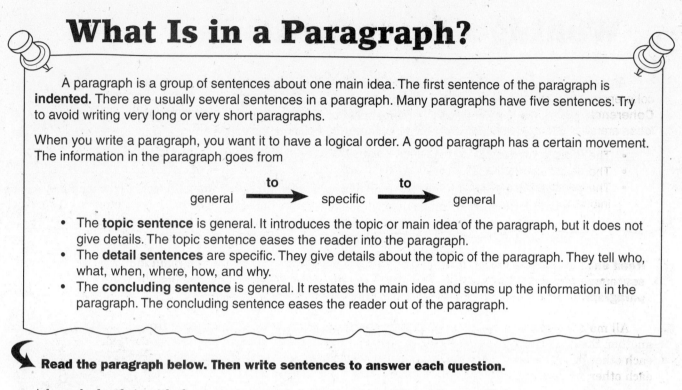

general **to** specific **to** general

- The **topic sentence** is general. It introduces the topic or main idea of the paragraph, but it does not give details. The topic sentence eases the reader into the paragraph.
- The **detail sentences** are specific. They give details about the topic of the paragraph. They tell who, what, when, where, how, and why.
- The **concluding sentence** is general. It restates the main idea and sums up the information in the paragraph. The concluding sentence eases the reader out of the paragraph.

Read the paragraph below. Then write sentences to answer each question.

A large body of air with the same temperature, pressure, and humidity is called an air mass. Air masses are produced when air remains over one part of Earth's surface for a long time. These great air masses move slowly across Earth's surface. These moving air masses take on the characteristics of the surface beneath them. Air moving over a warm surface is warmed, and air moving over a cold surface is cooled. Air moving over water becomes moist, and air moving over land becomes drier. As it moves, the air mass causes changes in the weather of an area.

1. What is the topic of this paragraph?

_____

2. Write the topic sentence from the paragraph.

_____

_____

3. Write a detail sentence from the paragraph.

_____

_____

4. Write the concluding sentence from the paragraph.

_____

_____

www.harcourtschoolsupply.com
© Harcourt Achieve Inc. All rights reserved.
 71
Unit 3: Building Paragraphs
Core Skills Writing 8, SV 9781419099014

Writing a Topic Sentence

A **topic sentence** introduces the topic or main idea of a paragraph. It tells what all the other sentences in the paragraph are about. The topic sentence is usually the first sentence in a paragraph, but it does not have to be in that position. A topic sentence should have **focus.** Focus means you have narrowed down the topic. For example, you might have the general topic of careers. You could focus on computers.

Knowing how to use a computer is an essential skill for everyone who wants to succeed in today's world. Computers can be used for many different purposes. One basic computer program that everyone should learn is the word processor. A word processor allows the writer to arrange and rearrange information easily, making the writing clearer and more accurate. Computers are also useful for accounting, programming, and graphic design. Jobs in the computer field are growing, and strong computer skills can serve you well now and in the future.

Read each topic below. Then choose a focus for each topic. Write a topic sentence that you could use to write a paragraph about your topic.

1. Topic: space exploration

Focus: _exploring other planets_

Topic sentence: _The exploration of other planets may someday lead to the colonization of space._

2. Topic: ocean tides

Focus: _____

Topic sentence: _____

_____

3. Topic: video games

Focus: _____

Topic sentence: _____

_____

 W R I T E   A W A Y

On another sheet of paper, write a paragraph using one of your topic sentences.

© Harcourt Achieve Inc. All rights reserved.

Writing Detail Sentences

The body sentences in a paragraph are **detail sentences.** Detail sentences give facts or examples about the topic. Details tell who, what, when, where, how, and why. Detail sentences help the reader learn more about the topic.

Choose your details carefully. Don't put a detail in your paragraph just because you think of it. A good plan is to list all the details you can think of. Consider what the reader needs to know about the topic. Then choose the three or four details that best support the topic sentence. Include the details in three or four body sentences.

     Knowing how to use a computer is an essential skill for everyone who wants to succeed in today's world. **Computers can be used for many different purposes. One basic computer program that everyone should learn is the word processor. A word processor allows the writer to arrange and rearrange information easily, making the writing clearer and more accurate. Computers are also useful for accounting, programming, and graphic design.** Jobs in the computer field are growing, and strong computer skills can serve you well now and in the future.

Complete the prewriting steps below. What does exercise make you think of? Write some details. Then, narrow your thoughts on exercise to the given topic sentence.

Topic: exercise

Details about exercise: _____

_____

_____

_____

Topic sentence (focus): Exercise can make you stronger physically and mentally.

Choose three best details from above for this topic sentence. Write three detail sentences that support the topic sentence.

_____

_____

_____

© Harcourt Achieve Inc. All rights reserved.

Writing a Concluding Sentence

A **concluding sentence** ends the paragraph. It restates the topic sentence in different words. It sums up the information in the paragraph. It can also explain what the information means. It may relate the information to the real world.

Imagine that your paragraph is a sandwich. The two slices of bread hold all the details inside—the mustard, the tomatoes, the pickles, the onion slices. The top slice of bread is the topic sentence. The bottom slice of bread is the concluding sentence. It is similar to the top slice but not exactly. The concluding sentence is like the topic sentence but not exactly. Read the paragraph about computers again. Notice how the topic sentence and the concluding sentence are similar but not exactly alike.

Knowing how to use a computer is an essential skill for everyone who wants to succeed in today's world. Computers can be used for many different purposes. One basic computer program that everyone should learn is the word processor. A word processor allows the writer to arrange and rearrange information easily, making the writing clearer and more accurate. Computers are also useful for accounting, programming, and graphic design. **Jobs in the computer field are growing, and strong computer skills can serve you well now and in the future.**

Read the paragraph below. Then write three possible concluding sentences for the paragraph.

Singers and athletes have much in common. Singers must practice breath control in order to sustain notes. In the same way, athletes, especially weight lifters, must regulate their breathing to lift heavy stacks of weights. Even though singers don't run races, they must have enormous stamina to project their voices without the aid of a microphone. Athletes must be in top condition, too, in order to compete successfully.

Concluding sentence 1: _____

_____

Concluding sentence 2: _____

_____

Concluding sentence 3: _____

_____

Name _____   Date _____

Prewriting a Paragraph

If only words would appear magically from your pen! Of course, they don't, so you have to go through a long process to write well. But you know that anything you want to do well takes time and practice.

Prewriting is a step when you think about what you will write. Prewriting is sometimes called **brainstorming.** Prewriting has three main chores.

- Think about your topic and audience.
- Choose your details.
- Organize your ideas.

Prewriting is an important skill to practice. Prewriting can take place in the seconds before you write a sentence or in the weeks before a big research project is due. When you prewrite, you work on ideas and words in your mind more than on paper. The Prewriting Survey on pages 115 and 116 can help you with your prewriting chores.

You have an assignment to write a paragraph about your favorite TV star. Do some prewriting. Think about what you must write. Fill in the chart below to help you prewrite.

Main goal of assignment: _____

My topic: _____

My focus: _____

My audience: _____

Details I might include: _____

_____

_____

_____

WRITE AWAY

Suppose you must write a speech to introduce your favorite TV star. Write 30 nouns, verbs, adjectives, and adverbs you might use to describe the TV star in your speech.

_____

_____

_____

_____

© Harcourt Achieve Inc. All rights reserved.

Voice

When you talk to others, they can tell how you feel by listening to your voice. In writing, **voice** is the way a writer "speaks" to the readers. Voice is how your writing sounds. The readers can "hear" how you feel about the topic. Think about the people who might read what you write. With your writing and the care you put into it, you can influence what they think and how they feel.

Your voice should fit your topic. To choose your voice for a topic, you must think of your audience. Your voice should also fit your audience.

What voice would you use to write about the death of a relative? _____

What voice would you use to write about your birthday party? _____

Follow the directions.

1. Name a topic you could write about using a humorous voice. Who would your audience be?

_____

2. Name a topic you could write about using a disappointed voice. Who would your audience be?

_____

3. Name a topic you could write about using a happy voice. Who would your audience be?

_____

4. Name a topic you could write about using a sad voice. Who would your audience be?

_____

5. Name a topic you could write about using an angry voice. Who would your audience be?

_____

6. Name a topic you could write about using a proud voice. Who would your audience be?

_____

WRITE AWAY

Imagine that your pet snake has slithered away. You must describe your feelings about the loss. Write a short paragraph about your feelings for your missing snake. Use a sad voice.

_____

_____

_____

_____

Writing Pattern: Main Idea and Details

Writing patterns can help you organize your work. Choosing a pattern in the prewriting step will help you choose a writing form. For example, suppose you want to give information about a topic. You would probably choose the main idea and details pattern.

You already know about main idea and details. The main idea is the most important idea in the paragraph. The details tell who, what, when, where, how, and why about the main idea. Details give a clearer picture of the main idea. When you choose this pattern, the Main Idea and Details Web on page 122 can help you plan your work.

Think about an important event in history. Suppose you have to describe it in an assignment. Use the Main Idea and Details Web on page 122 to write factual details about your important event. Follow the directions to complete the organizer.

1. What is the topic or main idea? Write it in the center oval.

2. What details can you use to tell about your important event? Can you tell who, what, when, where, how, and why? Can you use senses to tell about the event? Write one detail in each circle. Draw more circles around the center oval if necessary.

3. What are some words that expand each detail? Write specific adjectives, adverbs, and nouns that you could use to write a paragraph.

_____

_____

Use the Main Idea and Details Web to write a paragraph that gives factual information about your important event in history. Use another sheet of paper if necessary.

_____

_____

_____

_____

_____

_____

_____

_____

Writing Pattern: Summary

When you write a **summary,** or **summarize,** you tell the most important details about something. You tell who, what, where, when, why, and how. You might use this writing pattern if you want to give your audience a short description of a book, a story, an article, or a movie. You may need to summarize information for a research report.

- First, find the main idea of the selection. In a paragraph, the main idea is in the topic sentence.
- Then, decide on the key details about the topic. Don't tell all the details, only the most important ones.
- Finally, write the summary. Identify the topic, the main idea, and the key details.
- Write your summary in your own words. Don't look at the selection as you write the summary.

Remember, give the most important details so the audience understands the topic, but be brief. You can use the Summary Chart on page 123 to help you plan your work.

Read the paragraph below. Then complete the Summary Chart on page 123. Follow the directions below to complete the chart.

Matter is anything that has mass and takes up space. The three states of matter are solids, liquids, and gases. In solids, molecules are packed tightly together, vibrating slightly. For this reason, solids retain their shape. In liquids, molecules are packed less tightly; they slide over each other. Therefore, water has the characteristics of shape and movement. In gases, molecules bump against each other, moving wildly and quickly in all directions. Gas does not have its own shape and must take the shape of the container. These three states make up everything in the world.

1. Write the important details from the paragraph on the left side of the box. Tell who, what, where, when, why, and how. You do not need to write complete sentences.

2. Use the details from the left side of the chart to write a summary. Write complete sentences. Do not include any extra information. Write as few sentences as you can, but be sure to include all the important details.

Writing Pattern: Sequence of Events

Narratives and how-to directions tell events in order. In both kinds of writing, you would choose a writing pattern that shows the **sequence,** or order, of events. Suppose you want to tell someone how to make a grilled-cheese sandwich. You would write the steps in order. You would use the sequence of events pattern to tell what to do first, next, and last.

Be sure to tell the actions or steps in order. What if you were baking a pie? You would have a mess if the directions didn't tell you to put the pie crust in the pie pan first.

When you choose this pattern, a sequence chart can help you plan your work. It helps you think about each step. You can plan which **time-order words** to use. Some time-order words are *first, next, then,* and *finally.* You can make your own chart like the one below. Add as many boxes and time-order words as you need.

First,	Next,	Then,	Finally,

Can you cook or do crafts? What do you know how to do well? Write directions to tell someone how to do that thing. Those directions would use a sequence of steps. On another sheet of paper, draw a sequence chart to write the steps in order. Follow the directions below to complete the chart.

1. Which step is done first? Write it in the first box.

2. Which step is done last? Write it in the last box.

3. Which steps are done in between? Write time-order words on the boxes. Then write the steps. Draw more boxes if necessary.

Use the sequence chart to write a paragraph. Tell someone how to do the thing you have chosen. Use another sheet of paper if necessary.

_____

_____

_____

_____

_____

_____

_____

_____

© Harcourt Achieve Inc. All rights reserved.

Writing Pattern: Compare and Contrast

When you **compare** and **contrast,** you tell how two things are alike and different. If you compared the sun to the moon, you could say that both are objects in space and both can be seen from Earth. To contrast the two items, you could say that one generates heat and light and the other reflects light but does not generate heat. The sun and the moon are alike and different at the same time.

This writing pattern is useful if you want to inform your readers how two things are similar or different. When you choose this pattern, a Venn diagram can help you plan your work. It helps you think about how the two items are similar and different.

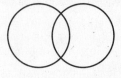

Compare and contrast two singers. Draw a bigger Venn diagram like the one above. Follow the directions below to complete the diagram.

1. Label each circle with the singers' names. Write the name of the first singer above one circle. Write the name of the second singer above the other circle. Write *both* in the part where the circles overlap.

2. Look where the circles overlap. Write words that tell how the two singers are alike in this space. For example, you might write *Both sing popular songs.*

3. In the circle under the first singer's name, write words that describe that singer. They should tell how the first singer is different from the second singer. Think about the singer's personality or behavior or style of music.

4. In the circle under the second singer's name, write words that describe that singer. They should tell how the second singer is different from the first singer.

Use the Venn diagram to write a paragraph. Compare and contrast the two singers you have chosen. Use another sheet of paper if necessary.

_____

_____

_____

_____

_____

_____

_____

_____

_____

_____

Writing Pattern: Cause and Effect

A **cause** is <u>why</u> something happens. An **effect** is <u>what</u> happens. For example, someone leaves the water running in a bathtub and the water overflows. In this example, the cause is the person's carelessness. The effect is that the bathroom is flooded.

The example above is a simple cause and effect event. However, one cause and effect pair can lead to a chain of cause and effect pairs. Think about the example above. Suppose the bathroom is flooded and the water leaks through the floor. The water soaks the ceiling underneath it. The water gets into an electrical socket and starts a fire. The entire house burns down, and the family has to stay in a hotel. All these new problems are caused by someone's failure to turn off the water in the bathtub. As you can see, each effect can lead to another cause. Each cause can lead to another effect.

This writing pattern is useful if you are telling why events happen. You must clearly state the cause and the effect so that a reader can understand why and what about an event. You can use the Cause and Effect Chart on page 124 to help you plan your work.

Think about a time you were careless. What problems did your carelessness cause? What were the effects of your carelessness? Use the Cause and Effect Chart on page 124 to explain the details. Follow the directions below to complete the chart.

1. Write the cause. Use exact nouns and verbs to explain the details.

2. Write the effect, or what happened. Use sense words so that the audience can "see" the effect.

Use the Cause and Effect Chart to write a paragraph. Tell about the time you were careless. Explain the causes and effects. Use another sheet of paper if necessary.

_____
_____
_____
_____
_____
_____
_____
_____
_____
_____
_____

www.harcourtschoolsupply.com
© Harcourt Achieve Inc. All rights reserved.

Writing Pattern: Problem and Solution

A **problem** is something that is wrong and needs to be fixed. A **solution** is the way to fix the problem. The problem and solution writing pattern can help you in persuasion. This pattern is useful to get the audience to agree with your solution. It can be used to explain something that is a problem. For example, you might discuss how hunger and sickness are big problems in this country and in the world. You could offer a solution to these problems.

When you use this pattern, be sure that the audience understands the problem. Identify the problem directly. Give examples and details that are clear and specific. Identify the solution directly. Explain why the solution works. When you choose this pattern, the Problem and Solution Chart on page 124 can help you plan your work.

Think about something that is a big problem in the world today. Use the Problem and Solution Chart on page 124 to list the details. Follow the directions below to complete the chart.

1. Identify the problem directly. Give an example or two, and list at least three details about the problem.

2. Identify the solution directly. Be specific. Tell how and why the solution would work.

Use the Problem and Solution Chart to write a paragraph. Identify a big problem in the world and give your solution. Use another sheet of paper if necessary.

_____

_____

_____

_____

_____

_____

_____

_____

_____

_____

_____

_____

_____

Focus on the Topic

A paragraph should have unity. That means all the parts of the paragraph work together to tell about one main idea. One way to get unity is to focus on the topic. Be sure your paragraph doesn't contain **unnecessary information,** or information that is not needed.

Pretend that you and four friends are sitting at a table. You're eating lunch, and everyone is happy to be together. The group is like a good paragraph. You announce the topic of conversation: "Did you hear about the trouble with the seventh graders?" (You're the topic sentence.) Three of your friends give details about the trouble. (They're the body sentences.) The fifth friend just nods and agrees with everyone. (He's the concluding sentence.)

Then your grandmother sits down at your table. She doesn't know anything about the topic. She is like unnecessary information in a paragraph. It doesn't belong with the other information. When you write a paragraph, focus on the topic and remove details that do not support the main idea. Be sure all the sentences in the paragraph support the topic sentence.

Read each paragraph carefully. Mark out the unnecessary information in the paragraph. Write why the information is not needed. Then rewrite each revised paragraph on another sheet of paper.

1.   Has your heart ever start pounding rapidly from anger? This pounding is one way your body responds to stress. Stress is a normal part of life. Breathing is a normal part of life, too. Stress can be caused by many different things. An argument with a friend, a test in school, or even loud noises can be stressful. Sometimes severe stress can make you ill. If you are constantly under stress, your blood pressure may rise and your digestion may be affected. If you are not under stress, you may have these medical problems anyway.

_____

_____

_____

2.   A fuse contains a thin strip of metal that acts like a protective switch. It stays closed (on) as long as there is not too much electrical current flowing through it. When there is an overload on the circuit and too much current flows, the fuse overheats and melts. The circuit is broken, and the current stops flowing. This can prevent a fire from starting at the place where the overload occurred. There was a fire in my house once, but I don't know if it started because of electricity. Once a fuse burns out, it cannot be used again.

_____

_____

_____

© Harcourt Achieve Inc. All rights reserved.

Revising

The goal of good writing is communication. You must write so other people can understand your meaning. Maybe you can read what you have written and know what it means. Gee whiz, you wrote it. You should know what it means. But will your reader be able to understand it, too? Will your reader gain a mental picture of your meaning? That's where revising comes in. **Revising** means "seeing again."

To revise, pretend that you are reading someone else's writing. Read it aloud. You want the writing to seem new and fresh to you. Ask yourself some questions about what you have read.

- Is the writing clear and direct?
- Are the sentences complete ideas?
- Are the verbs active?
- Are the adjectives and adverbs clear and exact?
- Do the conjunctions show the correct meaning?
- Does the paragraph make sense?
- How can this writing be improved?

The last two questions are the most important ones. If you write something and you can't understand it, your reader won't, either. You have to revise the writing until it makes sense. Revising means you must rewrite.

Read the following paragraph. It is not very well written. Revise the paragraph. To revise, you must do more than correct grammar errors. You can add details and change sentences. You must improve the writing and make it clearer for the reader. Use another sheet of paper if necessary.

    I remember the first time I visited my uncle's farm. There were some animals in the pastures, and some stuff was growing in the fields. We ate homegrown food. We went in the barn, where it was dusty, and saw some stuff hanging there. Down at the pond, we caught some fish and saw some birds. All in all, it was very educational, and I had a great time.

_____

_____

_____

_____

_____

_____

_____

_____

_____

_____

_____

_____

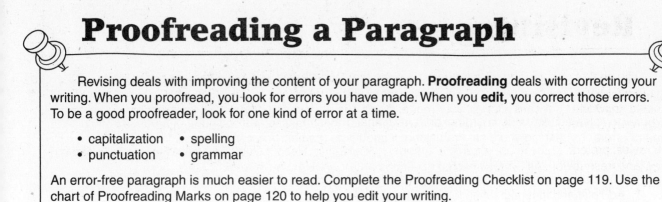

Proofreading a Paragraph

Revising deals with improving the content of your paragraph. **Proofreading** deals with correcting your writing. When you proofread, you look for errors you have made. When you **edit,** you correct those errors. To be a good proofreader, look for one kind of error at a time.

- capitalization
- spelling
- punctuation
- grammar

An error-free paragraph is much easier to read. Complete the Proofreading Checklist on page 119. Use the chart of Proofreading Marks on page 120 to help you edit your writing.

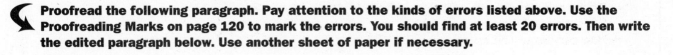

Proofread the following paragraph. Pay attention to the kinds of errors listed above. Use the Proofreading Marks on page 120 to mark the errors. You should find at least 20 errors. Then write the edited paragraph below. Use another sheet of paper if necessary.

Have you ever notised how hot the inside of a car gets in the sunlight. This is due to the greenhouse affect. Greenhouses are also heeted by the sun. glass lets the suns rays threw. Objicts inside the greenhous are heated by the sun's raise. Then, they radiate heat. This heat is trapped inside since it cannot pass through the glass. Carbon dioxide in the air can act like the glass on a greenhouse to trap heat carbun dioxide in the air lets the rays of the sun pass throuh. The sun's rays heat Earth. Some of this heat is radiated into the air. Carbon dioxide then traps some of this radiatd heat. Scientists are worryed that an increase in carbon dioxide in the air will increese the temperture of the air all over the wurld. Just a rise of a few degrees woud cause the polar ice caps to melt. Coastal areas could be floodid as a result.

_____

_____

_____

_____

_____

_____

_____

_____

_____

_____

Name _____   Date _____

Publishing

Once you have revised and edited your writing, you are ready to **publish** it. *Publish* means "to make public." In other words, you share your writing with others.

When you finish editing, write your final draft. Your final draft should be neatly written or typed. It should be free of errors. Try reading your final draft aloud. It should be the best you can write.

- Make a title page for your work.
- Think of a great title. Focus on words that you have used in your writing.
- Add pictures that might help to explain your topic.
- Use charts or bullets if needed to help your reader understand your topic.
- Be neat.

If you have done your best, the publishing part should be the most fun in writing.

Pretend that you have just finished a report on the greenhouse effect. Make a title page for your report. Include a title and some pictures. Use the space below for brainstorming if you need to.

© Harcourt Achieve Inc. All rights reserved.

Name _____ Date _____

Self-Evaluation: What's Going On?

In writing, there are two kinds of eyes—the writer's eyes and the reader's eyes. When you write, you use the writer's eyes. You see the words you are writing through the writer's eyes. When you read someone else's writing, you use the reader's eyes.

A good writer has both kinds of eyes. The writer uses the writer's eyes while writing. Then, to revise, the writer uses the reader's eyes.

A good writer can tell how good his or her writing is. Self-evaluation can help you tell how good a writer you are.

Write a paragraph below. Use another sheet of paper if necessary. You can write about your favorite book, your favorite memory, your favorite movie, or a topic of your choice. Be sure to include a topic sentence, detail sentences, and a concluding sentence. Do your best writing.

Then use the Self-Evaluation Checklist on page 121. Compare your paragraph to the checklist points. Check each point that agrees with your opinion of your writing. How good is your writing? What are the strengths and weaknesses of your writing? Do you have good control of the writing conventions? Do you have good word choice and sentence variety? Is your writing voice clear? What can you do to improve your writing? On another sheet of paper, write a paragraph that describes your writing style. Also write a paragraph that tells how you can improve your writing.

_____

_____

_____

_____

_____

_____

_____

_____

_____

_____

_____

_____

_____

© Harcourt Achieve Inc. All rights reserved.
Unit 3: Building Paragraphs
Core Skills Writing 8, SV 9781419099014

Writing a Description

When you **describe,** you paint a picture using words. You want the reader to "see" the thing you are describing. In fact, a good description lets the reader see, feel, hear, taste, or smell the thing. When you describe, you want to appeal to the reader's senses. The reader should feel as if he or she is with you examining the thing. Use vivid, concrete images. A concrete image is one that you can see in your mind, such as a blue dog. Remember to use your writing voice when you describe. You can describe persons, places, or things.

- When you describe a person, give unique details about the person. First, give an overall view. Then, give specific details.
- When you describe a place, give details that make the readers feel as if they are there. Provide a point of view from which to describe the place. Lead the reader through the place. Use movements such as front to back, top to bottom, or outside to inside. Try to give an emotional sense of the place. Use your writing voice.
- When you describe a thing, identify it in your topic sentence. Use sensory words as you describe. Pretend that your reader is looking over your shoulder.

   My grandmother's farm is still there, but it doesn't look the same anymore. Someone else moved in after my grandmother died, and now the pale white farmhouse is painted blue. The mulberry tree by the back door has rotted and fallen. The old weathered barn with its rusty tin roof has been torn down, and only my memories of how I used to play in it remain. The old smokehouse, where sausage used to hang, is gone now, too. The cornfield, where I used to run with the dogs or chase armadillos, has been replaced with a field of neatly trimmed green grass. The pigs in their muddy pigpens are missing, and so are the chicken houses. It's really not a farm anymore except in my memories.

Think of a person, place, or thing to describe. Then complete the graphic organizer below. Write the person, place, or thing in the circle. Write descriptive details on the lines. Use the graphic organizer to write a descriptive paragraph on another sheet of paper.

Writing a Narrative

When you **narrate,** you tell about a **sequence** of events. Often the sequence tells what happens in a story. A story is also known as a **narrative.** The narrative can be fact or fiction. A **personal narrative** is a story about something you have done. Write a personal narrative from your point of view.

- Use words such as *I, me,* and *my* to tell your story.
- Use your writing voice to tell the story. Include your personal feelings.

To write a narrative, follow these steps.

- Write an interesting beginning to "hook" the readers. Present your main **character** and the **setting.** Introduce the main character's problem.
- In the middle, give details about the main character's problem. Tell what happens in order. Use sensory details to make your story more realistic.
- Write an ending. Tell how the problem is solved. This is also called the **outcome.**
- Give your narrative a title.

To the Finish

I stood nervously at the water's edge with the other racers. I checked and rechecked my swimsuit and goggles. I stared across the lake, focusing on the finish line. I thought that might give me a competitive edge. But I was shivering instead, and I had no sensation of cold. We were all too scared to be cold. The crowd seemed noisy and restless, shouting out the name of one racer or another. Suddenly, everyone was still.

At the sound of the gun, there was pandemonium. The water churned with elbows, knees, and feet. I felt as if I was drowning. I couldn't catch my breath. I began to think of hanging back and letting the others take the lead. Then I could try to catch up. As I floundered, one of my old swimming rivals passed me. Now, with new determination, I set my course for the finish line. The familiar sound of water whooshing past my ears was reassuring. I found my rhythm and settled into it easily. Now all that mattered was passing the swimmers in front of me.

I felt as if I had been swimming for hours. I became disoriented, because I couldn't see anyone around me. Had the other swimmers left me so far behind? Had I strayed off course? Still I continued breathing, kicking, stroking, trying not to think. I could hear a distant roaring, or was it in my ears? I kept swimming and swimming. When my hand touched sand, I stood up shakily. The roar became cheers, and I realized I had won the race.

Write a personal narrative paragraph about a victory you have had. Include a beginning, a middle, and an ending in your narrative. Remember to indent the first line of your paragraph. Use another sheet of paper. Draw a picture to illustrate your narrative.

Dialogue

A narrative usually includes characters. Characters are real or made-up people or animals. They act in the events. Characters usually speak in narratives, too. What they say is called **dialogue.** When you write dialogue, you must follow some rules.

- Place **quotation marks (" ")** before and after the speaker's exact words.
- Use a comma to separate dialogue from the rest of the sentence unless a question mark or exclamation mark is needed. Any necessary comma or period goes inside the quotation marks.
- If dialogue is interrupted by other words, place quotation marks around the spoken words only.
- Begin a new paragraph each time the speaker changes.
- Be sure the dialogue sounds like real people talking. Avoid long speeches.
- Use the dialogue to tell what happens.

Wrong Number?

"Hello! Hello!" Jerome screamed into the phone receiver.

He got no answer, so he slammed the receiver back onto the phone. He had been sound asleep, and now he was just mad. But he tried to forget it and lay back down.

"Ring! Ring!" the phone shouted ten minutes later.

"Who is this?" Jerome yelled. "Why are you calling?"

Again there was no answer. Jerome jerked the receiver from his ear and stared at it, as if he could see who was on the other end of the line. But he couldn't, so he slammed down the receiver in disgust.

"Ring! Ring!" the phone shouted ten minutes later. "Ring! Ring!"

Jerome pulled himself from bed a third time. But this time he had a plan. Whoever was calling was about to get a deafening blast from his whistle.

"Tweet!" he blew into the receiver.

"Jerome?" he heard his mother's voice say. "Jerome, is that you? We must have a bad connection. We're in Europe, and there's a whistling sound on the line. Oh, dear, I just remembered that it must be late there. Is this a bad time to call?"

Jerome just fell back into bed.

Write a narrative about a wrong–number call. Include lines of dialogue in your narrative. Remember to put quotation marks before and after the dialogue. Begin a new paragraph each time the speaker changes. Use another sheet of paper to write your narrative. Draw a picture to illustrate your narrative.

© Harcourt Achieve Inc. All rights reserved.

90

Writing Poems

Poems are fun to write. You can play with words and tell your feelings. You can **rhyme** words and paint word pictures. Or you can write poems that don't rhyme—they are called **free verse.**

Rhyming words have the same sounds.

Dave—cave   write—right—night   no—throw—though

If you rhyme, think carefully about your word choices. Rhyming words receive extra attention, so they should tell something about the topic of the poem. Don't just rhyme because you can. Make your rhymes mean something.

- You can use **end rhyme,** words at the ends of lines with similar sounds.
- You can use **internal rhyme,** in which a word in the middle of a line rhymes with the end word.

Ambition

My father said as he tapped my head
And guided me into the foyer,
"Your head is thick, your mouth is quick—
Perhaps you should be a lawyer."

His voice was bland as he took my hand
And said, "You are not the smartest.
But you can draw, you have a strong jaw—
Perhaps you should be an artist."

He seemed a bit funny as he handed me money
And said, "The world is filled with rancor.
But you can add, you don't look half bad—
Perhaps you should be a banker."

He said no more as he showed me the door
And he firmly grasped the doorknob.
Then he kicked me out with a final shout,
"Perhaps you should look for a job!"

Answer the questions.

1. What kinds of rhyme are used in the sample poem?

   end and internal rhymes

2. Does the poem have a good title? Why or why not?

   Yes. The boy wasn't ambitous, but his dad was

W R I T E   A W A Y

Go to the library and look at a book of poetry. Write a few sentences describing the poems you read. Also write which poem you like best and why.

_____

_____

_____

_____

Writing Poems, page 2

When you write poems, you can experiment with language. You can mold the words in pleasant sentences. But remember, most poems are meant to be read aloud. So as you write your poem, read it aloud. Listen to the rhythm and sound of the words. Do the words flow or stumble?

To write a good poem, follow these steps.

- Choose a topic and a title for your poem.
- Decide if you will use rhymes or free verse.
- Use colorful words to paint a picture for your audience.
- Use rhyme and rhythm to help express your feelings.
- Use figurative language to compare things.

Think of a topic you would like to write about in a poem. Think of a title for your poem. Write some details to include in your poem. What rhyming words could you use in your poem? Then use your ideas to write a poem. Your poem should be at least eight lines long.

Topic: _____

Title: _____

Some details: _____

_____

Rhyming words: _____

_____

Title: _____

_____

_____

_____

_____

_____

_____

_____

_____

_____

_____

_____

Name _____ Date _____

The Five-Paragraph Essay: Introduction

Many papers that you write will contain five paragraphs: an **introduction,** three **body paragraphs,** and a **conclusion.** Like a paragraph, the five-paragraph essay moves from general to specific to general.

The introduction paragraph usually contains a general statement that introduces the actual topic of the paper. It should contain one or two more specific sentences about the topic that narrow it for the reader. Finally, the **thesis statement,** or statement of purpose, indicates a specific intent for the essay, in relation to the topic. The introduction in a structured five-paragraph essay clearly states the main idea in a thesis statement.

To write a good introduction paragraph:

- Introduce the topic in a general statement.
- Include a few specifics.
- State the main idea in a thesis statement.

     Though you might find it hard to believe, people have worked and fought for spices. Among the most valued spices are salt, pepper, and saffron. You may shower your french fries with salt or sprinkle extra pepper on your hamburger. You may enjoy the color and smell of saffron rice. Chances are, you don't give these spices a second thought. Nevertheless, throughout history people have made and spent fortunes for these spices.

Read the paragraph above. Then darken the circle by the best answer for each question.

1. What is the purpose of sentence 1?

    (A) introduce the topic

    (B) provide description

    (C) support a stated main idea

    (D) state the main idea

2. What is the purpose of the last sentence?

    (A) introduce the topic

    (B) provide description

    (C) support a stated main idea

    (D) give a thesis statement

3. What do the second, third, fourth, and fifth sentences do?

    _____

    _____

www.harcourtschoolsupply.com
© Harcourt Achieve Inc. All rights reserved.

Unit 4: Writing Forms
Core Skills Writing 8, SV 9781419099014

The Five-Paragraph Essay: Thesis Statement

A five-paragraph essay has a topic. It has a main idea. It also needs a thesis statement in the introduction paragraph.

- A thesis statement defines the topic for the whole essay. It tells the reader where the essay is going.
- It indicates the main idea and the particular focus of your topic.
- You recall that a paragraph has a topic sentence to tell what the paragraph is about. An essay has a thesis statement to tell what the essay is about.
- The thesis statement usually goes at the end of the introduction paragraph.

To write a good introduction, use one or more of these techniques:

- Open with a startling statement. Surprise and hook the reader.
- Introduce your topic by summarizing a piece of writing or events about your topic.
- Capture the reader's interest with a question.
- Include a thesis statement that lets the reader know what the rest of the essay is about.

Could Earth be the target of an asteroid? Asteroids, also called minor planets or planetoids, were first discovered in the early nineteenth century. They are small, irregularly shaped bodies that orbit the sun, most often between the orbits of Mars and Jupiter. Thousands of asteroids have already been discovered, and astronomers continue to discover more. Through their studies, scientists have learned about the origins, orbits, and sizes of asteroids.

Write the thesis statement in the above paragraph: _____

_____.

 Think about a topic related to outer space, such as a planet, a star, or space exploration. Then write an introduction paragraph for an essay about your chosen topic. Underline your thesis statement. Use another sheet of paper if necessary.

_____

_____

_____

_____

_____

_____

_____

_____

The Five-Paragraph Essay: Body Paragraphs

The developmental paragraphs, or **detail paragraphs,** are the body of the five-paragraph essay. The body contains three supporting paragraphs. Each body paragraph supports the thesis statement that you wrote in your introduction. Each paragraph has a topic sentence and details.

Each body paragraph discusses part of the main idea. When you plan your essay, you should divide your main idea into three parts. Then each part will have a topic sentence and details. Each part is one body paragraph. For example, you might write about asteroids. Your three parts could discuss the origins, orbits, and sizes of asteroids.

- In one body paragraph, you could discuss the origins of asteroids.
- Your topic sentence for this paragraph could be: Scientists have considered various theories about the origins of asteroids.
- Your details could include that asteroids may be parts of destroyed planets from the past or materials that did not come together to form planets.

To support your main idea, you need good details in your paragraphs. Details are facts that you use to support your topic sentence. When writing a descriptive paragraph, include specific details and arrange them in an order that makes the most sense for your purpose. Use precise and vivid words that will appeal to the readers' senses.

✎ **Do research on the origins of asteroids. You can use an encyclopedia, a book or magazine article, or the Internet. Write a body paragraph for the essay about the asteroids. Start with a topic sentence pointing out that scientists have differing ideas on the origins of asteroids. As details, discuss some of the different theories. Finally, write a concluding sentence. Use another sheet of paper.**

Your topic sentence: _____

_____

© Harcourt Achieve Inc. All rights reserved.

The Five-Paragraph Essay: Conclusion

Think of a five-paragraph essay as a big paragraph.

- Introduction = Topic sentence
- Body paragraphs = Detail sentences
- Conclusion = Concluding sentence

Most people don't know what to put in a **conclusion paragraph.** In the conclusion paragraph, the thesis is restated and a summary of key points that support the thesis statement is provided. Sometimes there is also an evaluation or speculation. There should never be new facts or details introduced in a conclusion. Just think of the three parts of a paragraph.

- In the topic sentence of your conclusion, restate the thesis statement or main idea. You don't want to repeat the thesis statement exactly. Use other words to make the same point.
- Include three details in the next few sentences. In the conclusion, you don't really need three detail sentences. You should provide a brief summary of the three body paragraphs. If you can recap the body paragraph details in a sentence or two, that's fine.
- Your concluding sentence should provide a way for you and your reader to get out of the essay. You can provide a link between the topic and the real world, for example. Your last sentence should be witty or clever or thoughtful or inquisitive. Here's your last chance to make an impression on the reader.

Review the sample paragraph from page 94 and your research from page 95. Then try the tips above to write a conclusion paragraph for an essay about asteroids. Use another sheet of paper if necessary.

_____

_____

_____

_____

_____

_____

_____

_____

_____

_____

_____

_____

_____

Writing a Comparison and Contrast Paper

In a **comparison and contrast** paper, a writer shows how two people, places, things, or ideas are alike and different. You can also write papers that only compare or contrast two things. To **compare** means to show how two things are similar. To **contrast** means to show how two things are different.

The Pueblo Indians and the Navajo Indians both wove cloth.   (compare)
The Navajos wove wool, but the Pueblos wove cotton and feathers together.   (contrast)

For a good comparison and contrast, you should have only two items. You should write at least three ways the two items are similar or different.

> **Read the comparison and contrast paragraph below. Then, answer the questions that follow. Write complete sentences.**

The wastelands of Antarctica and the Sahara in Africa are entirely different kinds of deserts. Antarctica is a continent that is virtually covered by an ice cap up to thirteen thousand feet deep. Summer temperatures rarely rise above 0 degrees Fahrenheit, and in winter, the temperature plummets to minus 70 degrees Fahrenheit. Antarctica is surrounded by miles of ice-encrusted ocean. In contrast, the Sahara covers a large area of North Africa and is made up of burning sand dunes and gravel. Daytime temperatures in the Sahara reach 135 degrees Fahrenheit in the shade. The Sahara is surrounded by land and sea. The thing that makes the two places alike is that they both receive about the same amount of rainfall.

1. What two things are being compared?

_____

_____

2. What is the main way the two places are similar?

_____

_____

3. What are two ways the two places are different?

_____

_____

_____

W R I T E   A W A Y

Think about a canteloupe and a watermelon. Brainstorm how they are similar and different below. On another sheet of paper, write a compare/contrast paragraph.

Similar	**Different**
_____	_____
_____	_____
_____	_____

Planning the Comparison and Contrast Paper

Here are some ways to write a good comparison and contrast paper. Remember, your paper should be five paragraphs long. You should have an introduction paragraph, three body paragraphs, and a conclusion paragraph.

- Think about your two items. Remember, do your prewriting to make your writing easier.
- Decide how the two items are similar. Decide how they are different. Choose at least three important similarities and differences. Use a Venn diagram to help you.
- Write a thesis sentence that identifies the two items being compared and contrasted.
- Explain how the two items are alike. Explain how they are different. Give examples.
- Each body paragraph should discuss one similarity or difference.
- Write a concluding sentence that summarizes the similarities and differences or gives a reaction to them.

Choose two items you want to compare and contrast. If you can't think of anything, compare and contrast houses and apartments. Draw a large Venn diagram like the one at the right. Follow the directions to complete the Venn diagram. Then use the Venn diagram to write a comparison and contrast paper on another sheet of paper.

1. Label each circle with an item name. Where the circles overlap, write *Both*.

2. In the Both space, write words that tell how the two items are alike.

3. In the first circle, write words that describe the first item. They should tell how it is different from the second item. Think about shape, size, and use.

4. In the second circle, write words that describe the second item. They should tell how it is different from the first item.

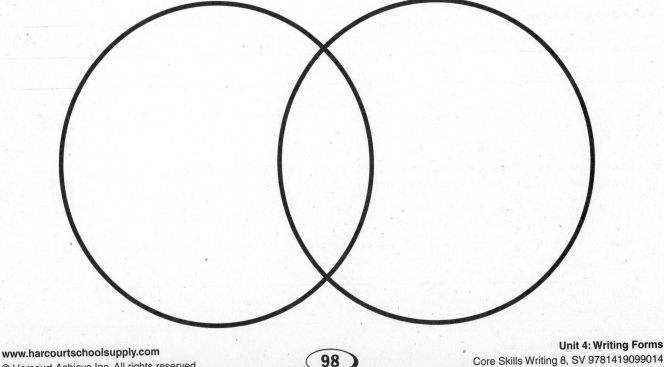

www.harcourtschoolsupply.com
© Harcourt Achieve Inc. All rights reserved.

Unit 4: Writing Forms
Core Skills Writing 8, SV 9781419099014

Name _____ Date _____

Writing a Persuasive Essay

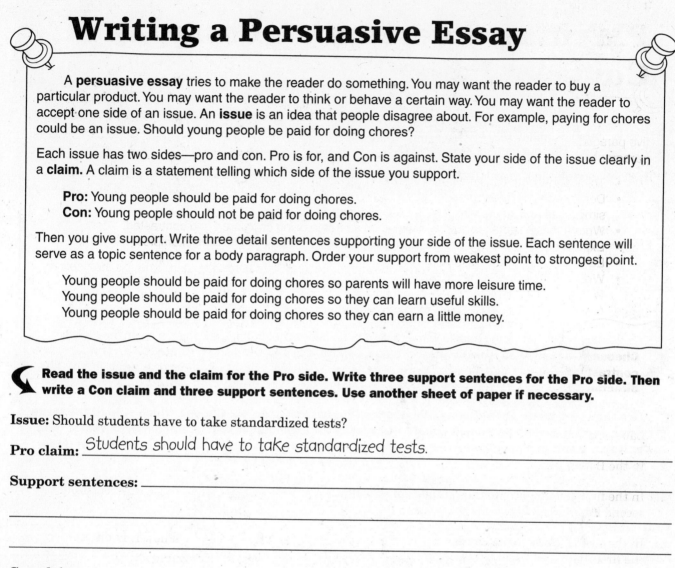

A **persuasive essay** tries to make the reader do something. You may want the reader to buy a particular product. You may want the reader to think or behave a certain way. You may want the reader to accept one side of an issue. An **issue** is an idea that people disagree about. For example, paying for chores could be an issue. Should young people be paid for doing chores?

Each issue has two sides—pro and con. Pro is for, and Con is against. State your side of the issue clearly in a **claim**. A claim is a statement telling which side of the issue you support.

Pro: Young people should be paid for doing chores.
Con: Young people should not be paid for doing chores.

Then you give support. Write three detail sentences supporting your side of the issue. Each sentence will serve as a topic sentence for a body paragraph. Order your support from weakest point to strongest point.

Young people should be paid for doing chores so parents will have more leisure time.
Young people should be paid for doing chores so they can learn useful skills.
Young people should be paid for doing chores so they can earn a little money.

Read the issue and the claim for the Pro side. Write three support sentences for the Pro side. Then write a Con claim and three support sentences. Use another sheet of paper if necessary.

Issue: Should students have to take standardized tests?

Pro claim: _Students should have to take standardized tests._

Support sentences: _____

_____

_____

Con claim: _____

Support sentences: _____

_____

_____

www.harcourtschoolsupply.com
© Harcourt Achieve Inc. All rights reserved.

Unit 4: Writing Forms
Core Skills Writing 8, SV 9781419099014

Writing a Persuasive Essay, page 2

When you persuade, you must think about your voice and your audience. You are trying to convince your readers. So, you must choose your words carefully. Think about the audience you are trying to convince. What do those readers care about? How can you persuade those readers? Remember, you don't have to convince people who already agree with you. You have to convince people who don't agree with you. You can appeal to your readers in three ways.

Personal appeal: Talk to your readers directly. Use words such as *I, me,* and *my* to write your persuasion. Address the readers as *you.* Make the readers like and trust you. Use your nicest writer's voice.

I think you will agree that paying young people to do chores is a good idea.

Emotional appeal: Play with your readers' emotions. Appeal to your readers' likes, dislikes, and fears.

If young people aren't paid to do chores, they might become lazy bums who can't support themselves in the future.

Logical appeal: Use facts and statistics to persuade your readers.

Studies show that young people who are paid to do chores get better–paying jobs when they leave school.

Use the same issue about taking standardized tests from page 99. Choose which side of the issue you support. Write a personal appeal to support your claim about taking standardized tests. Then write an emotional appeal and a logical appeal to support your claim. Use another sheet of paper if necessary.

Issue: Should students have to take standardized tests?

Your claim: _____

Personal appeal: _____

_____

Emotional appeal: _____

_____

Logical appeal: _____

_____

© Harcourt Achieve Inc. All rights reserved.

Writing a Persuasive Essay, page 3

Remember, your purpose in a persuasive essay is to make your readers agree with you. To write a good persuasive essay:

- Express your claim clearly in your introduction.
- Think about which appeals will work with your audience.
- Use your three strongest support points. Write a separate body paragraph for each support point. Give your weakest support point first and your strongest point last.
- A good concluding paragraph helps a persuasive paper. Restate your claim and explain why it is true. Stress the importance of your claim to the reader.
- Include a title that suggests your stance on the issue.

Carpooling Is the Way to Go

Traffic problems are getting worse and worse these days. Rush-hour gridlocks are lasting longer and longer. More cars are on the highways, and they need more time to go shorter distances. Too often, the cars are just sitting on the highways, their engines burning expensive gasoline and emitting pollution, their drivers getting angrier by the minute. Carpooling could solve many of these problems.

Gasoline prices have continued to climb. People are angry that they have to pay more for gasoline and still have to sit on the highways, wasting their precious fuel. It just makes sense that more people in a car means lower gasoline costs per person and fewer cars on the road. Carpooling can provide both of these solutions.

Many of our cities, even the smaller ones, are being choked by pollution. Most of this pollution is caused by cars. The more cars that are sitting on the highways with their engines running, the more pollution that is being produced. Carpooling could reduce the number of cars emitting these noxious fumes.

Cooperation is the cornerstone of success. Studies by citizen groups have shown that carpooling not only contributes to cleaner air, but it also means shorter commuting times. Shorter commuting times means fewer angry drivers. Unfortunately, getting people to cooperate has been difficult. The image of the independent driver, responsible to no one else, fades slowly. But people must be convinced that even one carpool can make a difference.

Everyone wants to pay less for transportation, to preserve our environment, and to improve our quality of life. Carpooling is one answer to those goals.

Choose one side of the issue about taking standardized tests on pages 99 and 100. Use your claim, your appeals, and your support points to write a persuasive essay about taking standardized tests. Be sure your claim is clear. Order your support points from weakest to strongest. Talk directly to your reader. Use another sheet of paper.

www.harcourtschoolsupply.com
© Harcourt Achieve Inc. All rights reserved.

Unit 4: Writing Forms
Core Skills Writing 8, SV 9781419099014

Writing a Literary Response

Sometimes you may be asked to write a **literary response.** You will have to read a story or poem and then tell your ideas about the selection. In a literary response, you must do more than list the facts of the story or poem. The facts would be the names of characters, where and when the story or poem takes place, and the events that occur. In a literary response, you will usually have to think more about *why* than about *what.*

- You may have to identify the main character of the story or poem.
- You may have to tell why a character does something instead of what the character does.
- You may have to identify the main conflict of the story.
- You may have to explain the main idea of the story.

Read the poem below. Then answer the questions. Write complete sentences.

The Night Has a Thousand Eyes
by Francis William Bourdillon

The night has a thousand eyes,
And the day but one;
Yet the light of the bright world dies
With the dying sun.
The mind has a thousand eyes,
And the heart but one;
Yet the light of a whole life dies
When love is done.

1. What do the first two lines of the poem mean?

_____

_____

2. What do the fifth and sixth lines of the poem mean?

_____

_____

3. What do the last two lines of the poem mean?

_____

_____

4. What feeling or mood is expressed by the poem?

_____

Writing a Literary Response, page 2

To write a good literary response, you should:

- support your answers by giving specific examples from the selection.
- support your answers by giving examples from your own experiences.
- connect main ideas or events throughout the selection.
- compare and contrast ideas in the selection to your own experiences.

Read the story below. Then answer the questions. Write complete sentences.

That Was That

It was my first funeral, and I didn't want to go. My grandmother had died, and I had loved her dearly, but I didn't want to see her in that coffin. My mother said I would be showing my respect to her memory by going. My father said it would be the last time I would get to see her. Doesn't he know she's dead? Why would I want to see her dead when I loved her alive? I wanted her alive, not dead. Couldn't they understand that? Then they said I had to go, and that was that.

At the funeral, I cried and cried. Everyone around me was crying, too, so I didn't feel so strange anymore. Her death had happened to everyone, not just me. Through my tears, I could see the sparkling colors of the church windows, and I felt at peace. I realized that death was just a part of life. My parents and friends would die someday. I would die someday. That was that.

At last I built up enough courage to go look at my grandmother lying in her coffin. At first I was scared, but then I kind of smiled. She seemed at rest, unlike the pain of her last days. I would miss her, I knew, but I think she was OK now. I had gone to my first funeral, and it was not as bad as I thought it would be. And that was that.

1. What is the character's feeling about death and the funeral at the beginning of the narrative?

_____

_____

2. What is the character's feeling about death and the funeral at the end of the narrative?

_____

_____

3. What didn't the character want to go to the funeral at first?

_____

_____

_____

4. What realization does the character make while she is at the funeral?

_____

_____

_____

5. The title of the narrative is "That Was That." The character repeats the statement three times. What do you think the author means by "that was that"?

_____

_____

www.harcourtschoolsupply.com
© Harcourt Achieve Inc. All rights reserved.
 103
Unit 4: Writing Forms
Core Skills Writing 8, SV 9781419099014

Writing for a Test

Do you like to take tests? Some people might, but most people don't. A test puts you under pressure. You usually don't have any control over what you must do, and then you're supposed to do your best! Many people especially don't like essay questions. Writing on a test can be easier if you follow these tips.

Prewriting (5 minutes)
- Is there a time limit? Is there a word limit? Are you supposed to write one paragraph or an essay? Are you allowed to use your textbook? Be sure you understand the directions and just what you are supposed to do.
- Read the essay question carefully. Do you understand it and your goal? Read the question again. If possible, read it aloud.

The school board is considering making students wear standard uniforms to school. They say wearing uniforms will help students to concentrate on their studies. What is your opinion? Write a persuasive essay for the school newspaper to convince others that your opinion is the correct one.

- Do not start writing immediately. Remember the prewriting step. You need to plan your writing. If you have 30 minutes to answer the question, spend 5 minutes prewriting. Then plan to spend 15 minutes to write and the remaining time to revise and edit.
- What are you asked to do in the question? What writing purpose and pattern should you use? Organize the topic in your head. If possible, write an outline of your answer.
- Put some ideas on paper. Freewrite your ideas and facts. Organize your information by numbering the facts in a logical order.

Organizing notes

Would school uniforms make students concentrate more on their studies? No.

Example of this: Students who didn't pay attention before wouldn't pay attention after uniforms.

Reasons why uniforms would not help:
1. There are other distractions besides clothes.
2. Making students wear uniforms would cause them to be angry, not studious.

What is a disadvantage of a school uniform? What is an advantage of a school uniform? Write your ideas. Use another sheet of paper if necessary.

_____

_____

_____

_____

_____

_____

Writing for a Test, page 2

Drafting (15 minutes)
- Now you are ready to write your first draft. You need a topic sentence or thesis statement. What focus do the details provide?
- Write the main ideas of the answer in the topic sentence or thesis statement.

Topic sentence or thesis statement

School uniforms would not make students concentrate more on their studies.

- Does the topic sentence or thesis statement capture your meaning? Is it a general statement of your ideas? Does it tell if you agree or disagree? If so, continue writing your answer. If not, revise your topic sentence or thesis statement.
- Remember to indent the first sentence in each paragraph.

Write

Now you are ready to write. Use your topic sentence or thesis statement and your organizing notes to write your answer. Be sure you stay focused on the topic and your stance.

Revising, Proofreading, and Publishing (10 minutes)

- Read what you have written. Then read the essay question again. Have you answered the question completely?
- Are there any facts you should include or delete?
- Is your grammar correct? Have you misspelled any words?
- Is your writing easy to read? Do you have time to rewrite?

Suppose you have been given the essay question about school uniforms on page 104. Write a paragraph that expresses your ideas. Use another sheet of paper if necessary.

_____

_____

_____

_____

_____

_____

_____

_____

_____

_____

_____

_____

_____

www.harcourtschoolsupply.com
© Harcourt Achieve Inc. All rights reserved.

Writing to Prompts

Many schools use tests to evaluate students' ability to write. One kind of test uses a writing **prompt,** which requires a written response to a statement, a question, or a picture.

- Read the prompt carefully to help you choose the purpose for writing, the audience, and the form and pattern for writing the essay.
- You may have to write using a time limit or a word limit, so remember to prewrite and plan.
- You may be supplied with paper to plan and write the response.

Complete the writing process for the prompt below. Write a short persuasive essay to express your ideas. Use another sheet of paper if necessary.

Prompt   Are you allowed to stay up as late as you think you should? What would you like your bedtime to be? Write a letter to convince your parents that you should be able to stay up later.

Organizing notes _____

_____

_____

Thesis statement _____

_____

Write _____

_____

_____

_____

_____

_____

_____

_____

_____

_____

_____

_____

_____

_____

_____

Name _____ Date _____

Writing an Informative Report

Are you ready for a challenge? Do you think you can write a report? Keep in mind that your report must be five paragraphs long. You need an introduction paragraph, three body paragraphs that give details, and a conclusion paragraph. Can you write that much? Well, let's give it a try.

First, you need to choose a topic and a focus. Suppose you are assigned to write a short report on objects in space. What would you do? You can begin the process by asking yourself some questions. Remember, this is the brainstorming or prewriting part.

What am I supposed to write about? _____

Can I write all about objects in space in 500 words? No, the topic is too broad. I need a focus. I need to narrow my topic.

What do I know about objects in space?

_____

_____

OK, now you have done a little brainstorming. Most work on an informative report is done before the writing begins. There are many things about objects in space you could write about. Let's try narrowing some topics.

objects in space $\longrightarrow$ planets $\longrightarrow$ Mars

objects in space $\longrightarrow$ smaller bodies $\longrightarrow$ asteroids

objects in space $\longrightarrow$ _____ $\longrightarrow$ _____

Let's say you are going to write a short report on asteroids. The first thing you need is a **thesis statement.** It tells what you will write about in the report. The thesis statement usually goes at the end of the introduction.

Thesis statement: Through their studies, scientists have learned about the origins, orbits, and sizes of asteroids.

Another possible thesis statement: _____

_____

Name _____ Date _____

Taking Notes

Let's say you are reading a **source** about your topic. A source is a place you get information. It may be a book, an encyclopedia, a magazine, a television show, or the Internet. There are many sources to consider for your report.

You find some information you want to use in your report. You decide to take notes. Two ways to take notes are **paraphrases** and **direct quotes.** You can also summarize the information you read.

- You use a paraphrase to restate someone else's ideas in your own words. A good paraphrase shows you are thinking about your topic. You are reading carefully.
- To paraphrase, you must first read the source carefully. Then close the source. Think about what you have read. Write your ideas using your own words.
- Copying words from a source and changing a few of them is bad paraphrasing. You must write the information in your own words. You must use your own voice and writing, not someone else's.

Carefully read the information in the sentences below. Next, put a sheet of paper over the sentences. Count to 50. Then write the information in your own words—two different ways! Use another sheet of paper if necessary.

Asteroids may be fragments of a planet destroyed in the far past, or they may be material that failed to condense into a single planet. Some scientists believe that asteroids may be matter from the nuclei of ancient comets.

_____

_____

_____

_____

_____

_____

_____

_____

_____

_____

_____

_____

_____

_____

_____

_____

_____

Direct Quotes

Sometimes the information you find is very important. You can't write the information better in your own words. Then, you can write a **direct quote**.

- A direct quote uses a group of words as they appear in the source. You copy the words exactly from the source. You put **quotation marks** at each end of the direct quote.
- If the direct quote includes the end of a sentence, the period goes inside the quotation marks.

One theory says that asteroids are "fragments of a planet" that was destroyed long ago. Some scientists believe asteroids are "matter from the nuclei of ancient comets."

Do not use many direct quotes in your report. If you do, then you are not doing much writing, are you? You are just copying someone else's writing.

Read the paragraph carefully. Answer each question by writing a direct quote from the paragraph. Remember to enclose the direct quote in quotation marks.

Asteroids vary greatly in size. The largest known asteroid is Ceres, which was discovered in 1801. The diameter of Ceres is about 600 miles. Other large asteroids include Juno, Pallas, and Vesta. Icarus, discovered in 1949, is one of the smallest known asteroids. Icarus has a diameter of just 0.6 mile.

1. What is the largest known asteroid? _____

_____

_____

2. What is the diameter of the largest known asteroid? _____

_____

_____

3. When was Icarus discovered? _____

_____

_____

4. What is the diameter of Icarus? _____

_____

_____

© Harcourt Achieve Inc. All rights reserved.

Name _____ Date _____

Documenting Your Sources

When you decide to use a source, be sure you gather all the publication data that you will need to **document** the source. In fact, you should gather this data before you take any notes. If you use the source material without using documentation to tell where you got the information, you are guilty of **plagiarism.** Plagiarism is passing off someone else's words or ideas as your own. Be sure, also, if you copy the source material word for word, that you enclose the material in quotation marks.

You document information in two ways. First, you include **citations** in your report. Citations are written in parentheses in your text. The citation points to the first word in the corresponding bibliography entry. So, the citation usually contains an author's name or a title and a page number.

Rule 1: When you introduce material without using the author's name, give the author's last name and page number(s) within parentheses.
Example: One of the smallest asteroids, Icarus, was "discovered in 1949" (Harris 191).

Rule 2: When you use the author's name in your writing to introduce material you used, give only the page number(s) within parentheses.
Example: As Jess Harris points out, the discovery of Ceres was made in 1801 (193).

Rule 3: If your source is an article without an author, use the title of the article in your citation. Include page number(s) in parentheses.
Example: The orbits of some asteroids bring them quite close to Earth ("Is Earth in Danger?" 86).

1. When should you gather publication data? _____

2. When would you be guilty of plagiarism? _____

3. What are citations? _____

Write a citation for each source.

4. Information from page 19 in a book by Sara Upholtz _____

5. Information from page 21 in an article called "Comets and Asteroids" _____
_____

Name _____   Date _____

Documenting Your Sources, page 2

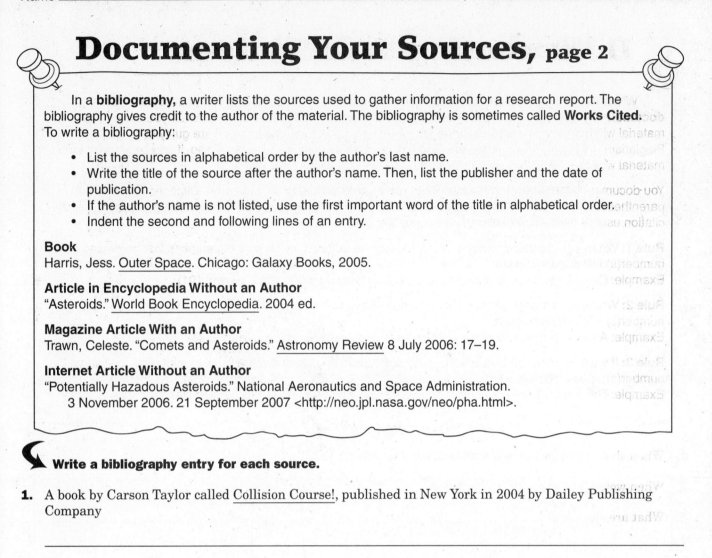

In a **bibliography,** a writer lists the sources used to gather information for a research report. The bibliography gives credit to the author of the material. The bibliography is sometimes called **Works Cited.** To write a bibliography:

- List the sources in alphabetical order by the author's last name.
- Write the title of the source after the author's name. Then, list the publisher and the date of publication.
- If the author's name is not listed, use the first important word of the title in alphabetical order.
- Indent the second and following lines of an entry.

Book
Harris, Jess. Outer Space. Chicago: Galaxy Books, 2005.

Article in Encyclopedia Without an Author
"Asteroids." World Book Encyclopedia. 2004 ed.

Magazine Article With an Author
Trawn, Celeste. "Comets and Asteroids." Astronomy Review 8 July 2006: 17–19.

Internet Article Without an Author
"Potentially Hazadous Asteroids." National Aeronautics and Space Administration.
    3 November 2006. 21 September 2007 <http://neo.jpl.nasa.gov/neo/pha.html>.

➤ **Write a bibliography entry for each source.**

1. A book by Carson Taylor called Collision Course!, published in New York in 2004 by Dailey Publishing Company

_____

_____

2. An article by Carla Brown called "Comets Are Coming," published on pages 35 through 38 in the March 27, 2007, edition of Space News Magazine

_____

_____

3. An encyclopedia article titled "Comets" with no author given, published in the 2002 edition of World Book Encyclopedia

_____

_____

_____

A Writing Plan: Outlining

You have been using writing plans for your paragraphs. You need a writing plan for your report, too. A longer writing plan is called an **outline.** It lists the main ideas of a topic.

- Start your outline with a thesis statement that tells the focus of the report.
- Next, write your main headings and subheadings. These parts tell what goes in each body paragraph of your report. Begin the first word in each line with a capital letter.
- Main headings start with a Roman numeral. Subheadings start with a capital letter. Each Roman numeral should represent a paragraph.
- Do not write a *I.* without a *II.* or an *A.* without a *B.*
- Write your report in the same order you have organized it in your outline.

Thesis statement: Through their studies, scientists have learned about the origins, orbits, and sizes of asteroids.

I. Origins

    A. Pieces of destroyed planet

    B. Pieces of planet that did not form

    C. Pieces of ancient comets

II. Orbits

    A. Most orbit between Mars and Jupiter

    B. Some orbits come close to Earth

    C. Asteroids may have hit Earth in past

III. Sizes

    A. Largest asteroid is Ceres

        1. Discovered in 1801

        2. Diameter of 600 miles

    B. Other large asteroids are Juno, Pallas, and Vesta

    C. One of smallest asteroids is Icarus

        1. Discovered in 1949

        2. Diameter of 0.6 mile

Answer the questions.

1. What would be the topics of the three body paragraphs?

_____

2. What would be a detail from the second body paragraph?

_____

Beginning and Ending a Report

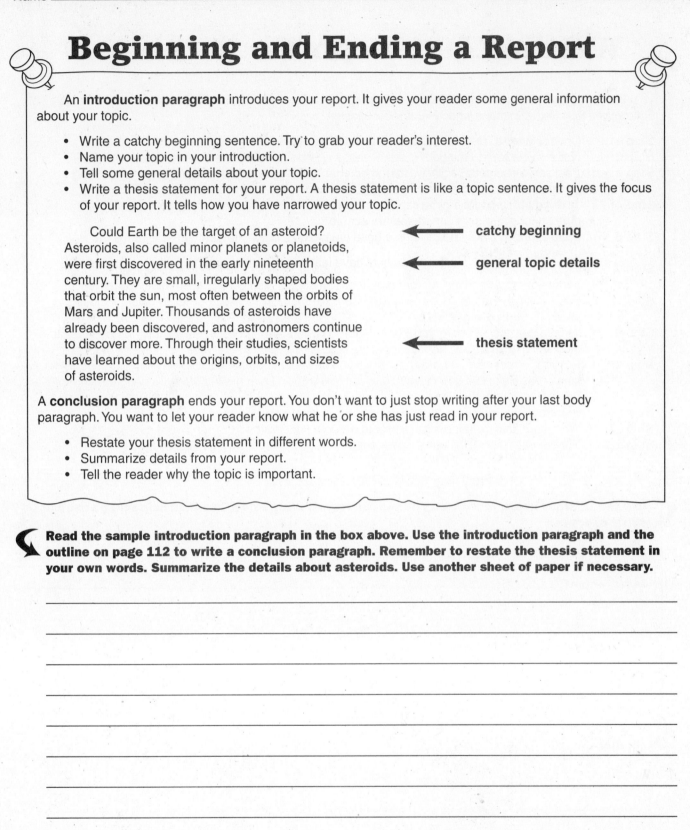

An **introduction paragraph** introduces your report. It gives your reader some general information about your topic.

- Write a catchy beginning sentence. Try to grab your reader's interest.
- Name your topic in your introduction.
- Tell some general details about your topic.
- Write a thesis statement for your report. A thesis statement is like a topic sentence. It gives the focus of your report. It tells how you have narrowed your topic.

    Could Earth be the target of an asteroid?   ←   **catchy beginning**
Asteroids, also called minor planets or planetoids,
were first discovered in the early nineteenth   ←   **general topic details**
century. They are small, irregularly shaped bodies
that orbit the sun, most often between the orbits of
Mars and Jupiter. Thousands of asteroids have
already been discovered, and astronomers continue
to discover more. Through their studies, scientists   ←   **thesis statement**
have learned about the origins, orbits, and sizes
of asteroids.

A **conclusion paragraph** ends your report. You don't want to just stop writing after your last body paragraph. You want to let your reader know what he or she has just read in your report.

- Restate your thesis statement in different words.
- Summarize details from your report.
- Tell the reader why the topic is important.

Read the sample introduction paragraph in the box above. Use the introduction paragraph and the outline on page 112 to write a conclusion paragraph. Remember to restate the thesis statement in your own words. Summarize the details about asteroids. Use another sheet of paper if necessary.

_____

_____

_____

_____

_____

_____

_____

_____

_____

© Harcourt Achieve Inc. All rights reserved.

Name _____   Date _____

Writing Your Report

Writing a good informative report takes a lot of time and hard work. You will do better if you have a plan. Follow the steps below to make writing your report easier.

Step 1:   Choose a topic. Think about your audience and your purpose.

Step 2:   Narrow your topic. Find your focus. Choose a writing pattern. Write a thesis statement.

Step 3:   Find some sources. Begin by looking up your topic in an encyclopedia. You can also search on the Internet. Record the names of your sources in a bibliography.

Step 4:   Take notes. Remember, you can summarize or paraphrase information. You can also write direct quotes. Be sure your notes are accurate.

Step 5:   Build a writing plan. An outline is a good writing plan. Each Roman numeral should be a paragraph in your report.

Step 6:   Write an introduction paragraph. Your introduction should have a catchy beginning. It should name your topic and include general details. It should also contain your thesis statement.

Step 7:   Write a rough draft of your body paragraphs. Remember to use your writing plan. Include citations if they are required.

Step 8:   Write a conclusion paragraph. Remember to restate your thesis in different words. You should also summarize details from your report.

Step 9:   Put your report aside for a day or two, if you have time. Then read it again. Read it aloud. What kind of revisions can you make? How can your report be improved? Do you need to add more details? Write another draft.

Step 10:   Proofread and edit your second draft. Make corrections.

Step 11:   Write your final draft. Be sure to proofread your final draft, too.

Step 12:   Publish your report. Include a cover sheet with a title and drawings if possible.

Use the 12 steps above to write an informative report. Start below, and then continue on another sheet of paper.

My topic: _____

Thesis statement: _____

_____

Name _____ Date _____

Prewriting Survey

> Purpose + Audience ⟶ Form

Purpose

1. What am I writing about?

_____

2. What do I want to say?

_____

_____

3. What is my purpose for writing? Explain.

_____

_____

Audience

4. Who will be reading my writing? What do I know about my audience?

_____

_____

5. What does my audience already know about my topic? What new information will I tell my audience?

_____

_____

6. How will I share my writing with my audience?

_____

_____

Prewriting Survey, page 2

Writing Purpose and Details

7. Why am I writing? Choose one purpose below and write the details you want to share.

To inform (to give facts about a topic)	Who What Where	When Why How

To express (to share a personal feeling or idea)	What I see What I hear What I touch What I smell What I taste

To entertain (to make the reader experience an emotion)	Feelings Memories Vivid words Figurative language Stories Poems

To persuade (to make the reader think or act a certain way)	My claim A detail that supports my claim A detail that supports my claim A detail that supports my claim

Writing Pattern

8. Which writing pattern will I use to achieve my purpose?

Main idea and details   Sequence of events   Comparison and contrast

Problem and solution   Cause and effect   Summary

Planning

9. Which graphic organizer can help me plan the details of my writing? Circle all that might be useful.

Main idea and details web   Sequence chart   Venn diagram

Summary chart   Problem and solution chart   Cause and effect chart

116

Writing Traits Checklist

Title _____

Trait	Strong	Average	Needs Improvement
Ideas			
The main idea of my writing is interesting.			
The topic is just the right size. I have good focus.			
The main idea is written clearly in one sentence.			
I have strong supporting details about the main idea.			
Organization			
The form of writing makes the information clear.			
My writing has a beginning, a middle, and an end.			
The details are in the right order.			
I use transition words to connect my ideas.			
My first sentence catches the reader's interest.			
My last sentence restates the main idea.			
Voice			
I show what I think or feel about the topic.			
I use the right tone for my writing: funny, serious, sad.			
I use words that my audience will understand.			
Word Choice			
I use the five senses to describe things.			
I use strong action words to tell what is happening.			
I use exact words in my writing.			
I use new words in my writing when needed.			

© Harcourt Achieve Inc. All rights reserved.

Writing Traits Checklist, page 2

Trait	Strong	Average	Needs Improvement
Sentence Fluency			
I have sentences that are short, medium, and long.			
I avoid repeating the same sentence pattern again and again.			
I use the same verb tense throughout the writing.			
I write sentences that begin with different parts of speech.			
Conventions			
All sentences begin with a capital letter.			
All my sentences end with the correct punctuation.			
All subjects and verbs agree with each other.			
All pronouns and nouns agree with each other.			
I use an apostrophe to show possession.			
I use a comma to join two independent clauses joined with *and, or,* or *but.*			
I use quotation marks to write dialogue or a quote.			
I indent the first line of each paragraph.			
Presentation			
My writing has a title.			
I use pictures, charts, or diagrams to support the ideas in my writing.			
The final copy is clean and neat.			
My drawing or writing is neat and easy to read.			
I have a cover and title page.			

Proofreading Checklist

You should proofread your work before you publish it. When you proofread, you look at your writing for mistakes. Proofread your work several times to search for mistakes. This list will help you proofread.

Capitalization

☐ Do all my sentences begin with a capital letter?

☐ Are titles and people's names capitalized?

☐ Are proper names of places capitalized?

☐ Are the months and days of the week capitalized?

Punctuation

☐ Does each sentence have the correct end punctuation?

☐ Did I use a period at the end of each abbreviation?

☐ Did I use a comma to separate items in a series?

☐ Did I use a comma correctly to separate a quotation from the rest of the sentence?

☐ Did I use quotation marks around dialogue?

☐ Did I use quotation marks around a direct quote?

☐ Did I use apostrophes to show possession?

Spelling

☐ Did I spell all the words correctly?

☐ Did I use a dictionary to check words that might be misspelled?

☐ Did I use a dictionary to check troublesome words?

Grammar and Usage

☐ Do my subjects and verbs agree in number?

☐ Do my nouns and pronouns agree in number?

☐ Do I have any sentence fragments?

☐ Do I have any run-on sentences?

☐ Do I have any double negatives?

Name _____ Date _____

Proofreading Marks

↰ **Use the marks below to edit your writing.**

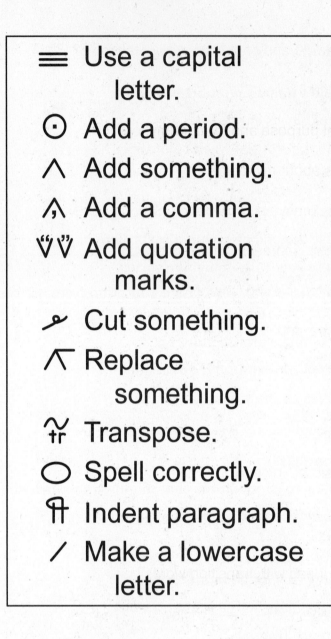

≡ Use a capital letter.

⊙ Add a period.

∧ Add something.

⩔ Add a comma.

ᐯᐯ Add quotation marks.

⸜ Cut something.

∧ Replace something.

⭑ Transpose.

◯ Spell correctly.

¶ Indent paragraph.

/ Make a lowercase letter.

www.harcourtschoolsupply.com
© Harcourt Achieve Inc. All rights reserved.

Blackline Masters
Core Skills Writing 8, SV 9781419099014

Name _____ Date _____

Self-Evaluation Checklist

Title _____

		Yes	No

1. Did I take time to prewrite and brainstorm about my topic? _____ _____

2. Did I think about my audience? _____ _____

3. Did I choose the right purpose and form for my topic? _____ _____

4. Do I have good focus about my topic? _____ _____

5. Is my writing clear and easy to understand? _____ _____

6. Is the main idea of each sentence clear and direct? _____ _____

7. Did I present information in a logical order? _____ _____

8. Did I choose interesting and exact words? _____ _____

9. Are my verbs and adjectives lively and interesting? _____ _____

10. Did I add details, examples, facts, explanations, or direct quotes to strengthen my writing? _____ _____

11. Did I remove unnecessary information? _____ _____

12. Did I follow basic rules for capitalization, punctuation, spelling, grammar, and usage? _____ _____

13. Did I link events and ideas with transition words? _____ _____

14. Do my sentences have good rhythm and flow? _____ _____

15. Did I revise confusing parts to make them clearer? _____ _____

16. Did I choose a title that grabs my reader's attention? _____ _____

17. Is my writing neat and easy to read? _____ _____

18. Have I done my best work on this piece of writing? _____ _____

www.harcourtschoolsupply.com
© Harcourt Achieve Inc. All rights reserved.

Blackline Masters
Core Skills Writing 8, SV 9781419099014

/ copy

Date _____

Main Idea and Details Web

➤ **Write the main idea in the oval. Write five strong details in the circles. Think about specific and lively words that you could use in your writing to tell about the details. Write these words in the rectangles.**

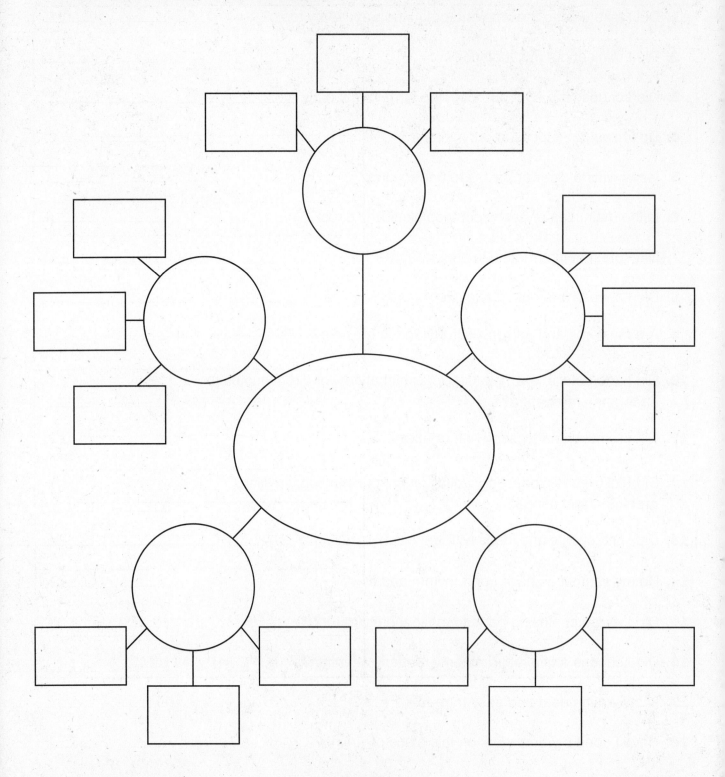

Summary Chart

Write the details on the left side of the chart. Write a summary on the right side of the chart. Try to include all the information in as few sentences as you can.

Who	Summary
	_____
	_____
What	_____
	_____
Where	_____
	_____
	_____
	_____
When	_____
	_____
	_____
Why	_____
	_____
	_____
How	_____
	_____

© Harcourt Achieve Inc. All rights reserved.

Problem and Solution Chart

⟵ **Name the problem in the first box. Then write details about the problem. Name the solution that would fix the problem. Give details to explain why the solution would work.**

Problem	Details about Problem *(Why is it a problem?)*

Solution	Details about Solution *(Why is it a good solution?)*

Cause and Effect Chart

⟵ **Write what happened in the Effect box. Write the reason it happened in the Cause box.**

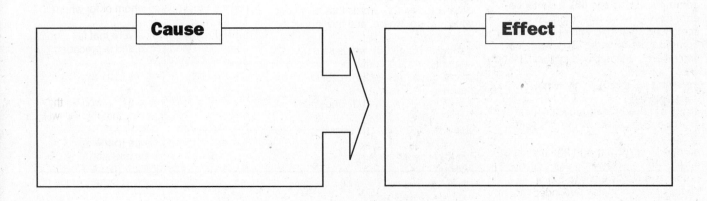

Cause   **Effect**

Glossary

action verb (page 14) a verb that shows action

active verb (page 55) a verb that shows action done by the subject of the sentence

adjective (page 15) a word that modifies a noun or pronoun

adjective phrase (page 38) a prepositional phrase that serves as an adjective

adverb (page 15) a word that modifies a verb, an adjective, or another adverb

adverb phrase (page 38) a prepositional phrase that serves as an adverb

antecedent (page 13) the noun for which a pronoun stands

audience (page 10) the ones who will read what you write

bibliography (page 111) a list of sources for a research report

body paragraphs (page 93) paragraphs between the introduction and conclusion in an essay that give details about the main idea

brainstorming (page 17) to think about ideas for your writing

cause (page 81) why something has happened

character (page 89) real or made-up people or animals in a narrative

citation (page 110) information in parentheses in your report that tells about your sources

claim (page 99) a statement about which side of the issue you support

clause (page 36) a group of related words that includes a subject and a predicate

coherence (page 70) when the parts of a paragraph have a logical order

comma (page 52) a mark of punctuation used to separate the parts of a compound sentence or a series

comma splice (page 66) a sentence error caused when two complete sentences are joined with only a comma

common noun (page 13) a word that names any person, place, or thing; begins with a small letter

compare (page 80) to show how two things are alike

complete predicate (page 23) the simple predicate and all the words that describe it

complete subject (page 23) the simple subject and all the words that describe it

complex sentence (page 52) a sentence that contains one independent clause and one or more dependent clauses

compound object (page 44) an object containing two or more direct objects

compound predicate (page 44) a predicate containing two or more simple predicates

compound sentence (page 52) a sentence that is made up of two or more simple sentences

compound subject (page 44) a subject containing two or more simple subjects

concluding sentence (page 70) restates the main idea and summarizes the information in the paragraph

conclusion paragraph (page 93) the last paragraph in a report or long piece of writing

conjunction (page 16) a word that connects words or groups of words

connective (page 16) a word that joins parts of a sentence

contrast (page 80) to show how two things are different

conventions (page 21) the rules of grammar and writing

coordinate conjunction (page 16) a conjunction that joins two words, two phrases, or two clauses of equal rank

correlative conjunction (page 43) a pair of conjunctions that joins pairs of ideas

dangling modifier (page 67) a modifier that has no word in the sentence to modify

declarative sentence (page 50) a sentence that makes a statement

dependent clause (page 36) a clause that is not a complete sentence; it must be attached to an independent clause

describe (page 88) to tell what something is like; to paint a picture with words

detail paragraphs (page 95) the body paragraphs in an essay

detail sentences (page 70) body sentences that tell more about the main idea of a paragraph

details (page 31) words that tell whose, which, when, where, and how about the main idea

dialogue (page 90) words said by characters in a narrative

direct object (page 26) receiver of the action in a sentence

direct quote (page 108) copying words exactly from a source

document (page 110) to give publication information about a source

draft (page 22) a version of a piece of writing

drafting (page 17) writing a version of your ideas on a topic

edit (page 22) to correct errors you have made in writing

effect (page 81) something that has been caused to happen

emphasis (page 70) when the important ideas in a paragraph are stressed

end rhyme (page 91) words at the end of lines of a poem that have similar sounds

entertain (page 11) to please or amuse the reader

exclamation mark (page 50) a mark of punctuation used at the end of an exclamatory sentence

exclamatory sentence (page 50) a sentence that shows excitement or strong feeling

express (page 11) to tell your personal feelings

figurative language (page 60) words used to compare unlike things

focus (page 72) to narrow a topic

free verse (page 91) a kind of poem that does not rhyme

fused sentence (page 65) a sentence error caused when two complete sentences are joined with no mark of punctuation

future tense verb (page 56) a verb that tells what will happen in the future

gerund (page 39) a verb that ends in *ing* and functions as a noun

helping verb (page 27) a verb that comes before the main verb in a sentence

ideas (page 19) what you have to say or write about a topic

imperative sentence (page 50) a sentence that makes a request or gives a command

indent (page 71) move in five spaces from the left margin

independent clause (page 36) a clause that is a complete sentence and shows a complete thought

indirect object (page 42) the noun or pronoun that tells to whom or for whom an action is done

infinitive (page 40) a verb that functions as a noun or adjective and is preceded by *to*

inform (page 11) to tell facts about a topic

internal rhyme (page 91) a word in the middle of a line of poetry that rhymes with the end word

interrogative sentence (page 50) a sentence that asks a question

introduction paragraph (page 93) the first paragraph in a report or long piece of writing

inverted order (page 61) changing the order of the subject and the verb in a sentence

issue (page 99) an idea that people disagree about

© Harcourt Achieve Inc. All rights reserved.

Core Skills Writing 8, SV 9781419099014

journal (page 12) a record of daily events

linking verb (page 28) a verb that links the subject to a noun or an adjective in the complete predicate

literary response (page 102) writing your ideas about a literary reading selection

main idea (page 24) what a piece of writing is mainly about

metaphor (page 60) figurative language that compares two things by speaking of one thing as if it were another; does not use *like* or *as*

misplaced modifier (page 67) a modifier placed in the wrong position in a sentence so that its meaning is unclear

modifier (page 15) a word or group of words that changes the meaning of another word

narrate (page 89) tell about a sequence of events

narrative (page 89) a factual or fictional story

noun (page 13) a word that names a person, place, or thing

object of the preposition (page 37) the noun or pronoun that follows a preposition

object pronoun (page 13) used as the object of a sentence

organization (page 19) the way you arrange the ideas you are writing

outcome (page 89) the ending of a narrative

outline (page 112) a writing plan for the content of a report

paragraph (page 70) a group of sentences that tells about one main idea

paraphrase (page 108) to restate someone else's ideas in your own words

participle (page 41) a form of a verb used as an adjective to modify a noun or pronoun

passive verb (page 55) a verb that shows being and not action

past tense verb (page 56) a verb that tells what happened in the past

period (page 50) a mark of punctuation used at the end of a declarative sentence

personal narrative (page 89) a story about something you have done

personification (page 60) giving human qualities to nonhuman things

persuade (page 11) to try to convince the reader to do something

persuasive essay (page 99) tries to make the reader do something

phrase (page 36) a group of words that does not have a subject or a predicate

plagiarism (page 110) passing off someone else's words or ideas as your own

plural verb (page 25) a verb that agrees with a plural subject

poem (page 91) a composition in verse that may or may not use rhyming words

predicate (page 23) the part of a sentence that tells what the subject is or does

predicate adjective (page 28) an adjective linked to a subject by a linking verb

predicate nominative (page 28) a noun or pronoun linked to a subject by a linking verb

preposition (page 16) a word that shows the relation of a noun or pronoun to another word in a sentence

prepositional phrase (page 37) a phrase made up of a preposition, its object, and any other words

present tense verb (page 56) a verb that tells what is happening now

presentation (page 21) the way words and pictures look on the page

prewriting (page 17) to think about what and why you are writing

problem (page 82) something that is wrong

prompt (page 106) a question or situation given as a writing assignment

pronoun (page 13) a word that takes the place of a noun

proofreading (page 18) searching for errors you have made in writing

proper noun (page 13) a word that names a particular person, place, or thing; begins with a capital letter

publishing (page 18) sharing your writing with others

purpose (page 11) your reason for writing

question mark (page 50) a mark of punctuation used at the end of an interrogative sentence

quotation marks (page 90) punctuation marks that are placed at each end of dialogue or a direct quote

relative pronoun (page 48) a pronoun that relates an adjective clause to the noun or pronoun the clause modifies

revising (page 18) to think more about what you have written to make it better

rhyme (page 91) to have similar sounds

rhyming words (page 91) words that have similar sounds

run-on sentence (page 65) a sentence error caused by incorrect punctuation

sentence (page 23) a group of words that tells a complete thought

sentence fluency (page 21) the rhythm and flow of your sentences

sentence fragment (page 64) a part of a sentence that does not tell a complete idea

sequence (page 79) a series of events in order

series (page 53) a list of three or more words or items

setting (page 89) where and when the events of a narrative take place

simile (page 60) figurative language that compares two things by using *like* or *as*

simple predicate (page 24) the main verb in the complete predicate

simple sentence (page 52) a complete sentence that contains only one complete thought

simple subject (page 24) the main noun or pronoun in the complete subject

singular verb (page 25) a verb that agrees with a singular subject

solution (page 82) the way to fix a problem

source (page 108) a place to find information

subject (page 23) who or what a sentence is about

subject pronoun (page 13) used as the subject of a sentence

subordinate clause (page 47) another name for a dependent clause

subordinate conjunction (page 16) a conjunction that joins a dependent clause to an independent clause

summarize (page 78) to tell the key details of an event or a piece of writing

summary (page 78) the key details of a piece of writing

tense (page 56) the time a verb tells

thesis statement (page 93) a sentence that tells the focus of a report or long piece of writing

time-order words (page 79) transition words that show movement in time

topic (page 17) what you are writing about

topic sentence (page 70) tells the main idea of the paragraph

understood subject (page 50) the subject (*you*) of an imperative sentence that does not appear in the sentence; however, the subject is understood to be *you*

unity (page 70) when all the parts of a paragraph tell about one main idea

unnecessary information (page 83) information that does not belong in a paragraph

verb (page 14) a word that shows action or connects the subject to another word in a sentence

verb phrase (page 27) the main verb and its helpers in a sentence

verb tense (page 56) the time a verb tells

verbal (page 39) a verb form used as another part of speech

voice (page 20) the way a writer "speaks" to the reader through writing

word choice (page 20) the words you pick to express your ideas

writing traits (page 19) skills, features, or characteristics of writing

© Harcourt Achieve Inc. All rights reserved.

Core Skills Writing 8, SV 9781419099014